The Trail of Tamerlane

By the same author

Cucumber Sandwiches in the Andes
Prince Henry the Navigator

JOHN URE

The Trail of Tamerlane

CONSTABLE LONDON

First published in Great Britain 1980
by Constable and Company Ltd
10 Orange Street London WC2H 7EG
Copyright © 1980 by John Ure
Set in Monotype Bembo 12pt
Printed in Great Britain by The Anchor Press Ltd
and bound by Wm Brendon & Son Ltd
both of Tiptree, Essex

British Library cataloguing in publication data
Ure, John
The trail of Tamerlane
1 Iran – Description and travel
2 Turkey – Description and travel – 1960–
I Title
915.5'04'5   DS259
ISBN 0 09 463350 9

For Alasdair Hugo
who has not yet been
strapped on to a camel

Contents

Illustrations

9

Where not otherwise stated, all photographs are by Caroline Ure

The Persian Dynasties

with dates of some of the rulers mentioned in the book

ACHAEMENIANS 640–323 BC
Darius 521–485
Xerxes I 485–465
(joint builders of Persepolis)

SELEUCIDS 323–223 BC

PARTHIANS 223 BC–225 AD

SASSANIANS 225–642

Islamic invasion and instability 642–1037

SELJUKS 1037–1220
(builders of the Cifte Minareli Medrese at Erzurum and
the Turbes at Ahlât)

MONGOLS 1220–1380
First and second Mongol invasions
followed by successive rulers including:
Hulagu 1256–1265
(founder of the Kingdom of Hulagu and suppressor of the
Assassins)
Oljeitu 1304–1316
(builder of Sāltīnoyeh)

TIMURIDS 1380–1500
Timur (Tamerlane) 1380–1405

SAFAVIDS 1500–1736
Shah Abbas 1587–1629
(builder of much of Isfahan)

Interregnum 1736–1787

QAJARS 1787–1925

PAHLAVIS 1925
Reza Shah 1925–1941
Mohammed Reza 1941 (and still on Peacock Throne at date of journey described in this book)

Author's Note

The journey described in this book was made shortly before the recent revolution in Iran; indeed, it would have been impossible to have made it in the immediate aftermath of those events. My remarks about the troubled history of the Kurds and Kurdistan take no account of recent developments, and anyone who looks in these pages for political commentary on events later than the fourteenth century will look in vain. Like many of the previous travellers whom I quote or describe, I focused my attention on those characteristics of the regions I traversed which survive the upheavals of particular moments in history.

Many people helped me make this journey and write this book, among them all those who befriended us along the route and only some of whom I have been able to mention in the text. I am grateful to all of them.

I also wish especially to thank Sir Denis Wright GCMG, a one-time (and long-time) British Ambassador in Iran and also a former consul in Eastern Turkey, who not only gave us invaluable advice and encouragement before we set out, but after our return had the kindness and patience to read my manuscript and make a number of helpful suggestions and an even greater number of necessary corrections. The failures that remain are all my own.

My wife's contribution to this book is far more than the photographs. At those moments when what had been planned as a light-hearted adventure seemed to have led us into less light-hearted dangers, it was she who provided the greater part of whatever fortitude was demanded of us. She also kept a sense of humour when all around were losing theirs. He who still has such a companion when the journey is over is truly fortunate.

ARAL
SEA

CENTRAL ASIAN
RUSSIA

Bukhara

Samarkand

Oxus

SEA

sāvar

burz Mts

n'

PERSIA

AFGHANISTAN

Isfahan

ASHQAI COUNTRY

Persepolis

Shīrāz

0   100   300   miles

Chapter 1

The Call of the Camel Bells

There comes a moment when any man asks himself what the devil he is doing, and I had reached that moment. I was lost in a strange land and nightfall was approaching. I was hungry and my provisions had fallen unobserved from my saddle somewhere behind me on the Persian plains. My throat was dry and felt as if it would provide a good surface on which to strike matches. My sole means of transport – a camel of unappealing personal habits, called Zenocrate – had just made a determined effort to bite off my left knee-cap. My only human companion was rapidly losing her normal sang-froid and was only slightly less unfriendly than Zenocrate in her manner towards me: she did not threaten my knee-caps but she did bite off my head every time I spoke. I had sand in my hair, my socks, my money belt and apparently (since it had stopped) in my wrist-watch. Why had I – a comfort-loving diplomat – allowed myself to get into this absurd predicament?

The answer was that I had allen under the spell of a region and of a man. The region was a loosely defined one, unified by contiguity rather than by geological formation, by romantic associations rather than by natural frontiers, by its invaders rather than by its residents. It was the land across which the ancient Silk Road wound its way between East and West. It was the land of Hassan, of camel trains riding forth at evening from the wells, of caravanserais crowded with merchants and pilgrims. It was the land of Sohrab and Rustum, of solemn wastes on which were enacted mighty feats of arms, of the Oxus rolling silently into the Aral Sea. It was a land where carpets are currency and where a stout horse is prized above rubies. It was a region of cities whose names beat like bells along the golden road: Trebizond and Erzurum, Persepolis and Isfahan, Mashhad and Samarkand. It was all that tract of Asia which stretches from the Turkish plains of Anatolia, past the blue mountain peaks of the Caucasus, across the uplands of Persia to the baking deserts of Central Asia. This was the region under whose spell I had fallen.

And the man who shared in casting this spell was the man who above all others had made this quarter of the world his oyster. Tamburlaine the Great, Tamerlane the Conqueror, Timur the Lame . . . call him what you will, it was he who at the end of the fourteenth century A.D. had stamped his ferocious imprint on my region. There had been others who had marched this way and laid claim to suzerainty of this quarter of the globe. Darius the Great had extended the bounds of Persia to cover much of this territory in the fifth century B.C.; a century and a half later, Alexander had crossed the Hellespont to traverse Asia Minor and Persia on his way to India; in the twelfth century A.D., Genghis Khan had pushed the boundaries of his Mongol empire westwards until it reached the Black Sea; in the decades before Tamerlane, the Golden Horde had intermittently ravaged extensive parts of the region. But no one had pushed out in all directions with quite the acquisitive and wanton energy of Tamerlane. Although he had been a transient ruler, at the height of his power he had made his Tartar writ run throughout the length and breadth of the far-flung domains reaching out from his capital at Samarkand. Tamerlane had also campaigned beyond my region – into the steppes of Russia and to the banks of the Ganges – but over these outer regions he did not attempt to maintain his sway. It was as if he, like me, felt that the kernel of the world lay around the Aral, the Caspian and the Euxine seas.

The spell of the region may be easier to impart than the spell of the man. Tamerlane's hold on the imagination is the grip of a monster. It has always been so. Christopher Marlowe's hero repelled but fascinated the Elizabethan court and has exerted the same effect on generations of Englishmen ever since. Everything about him is larger than life. His courage was legendary, even among Tartar warriors renowned for their courage: he shed his armour in the thick of the battle more than once – thereby suffering arrow wounds – because he thought that others might be afraid. But Tamerlane's cruelty was no less notorious than his valour: he buried opponents alive, built minarets of skulls, and put countless cities to the sword. His impatience was terrifying: he hanged governors who had been tardy in their work and he personally supervised the building – night and day – of public monuments to grace his capital. His energy was phenomenal: he campaigned incessantly and feasted unrestrainedly after each expedition. Marlowe captures the mood of all this feverish activity:

> I'll have you learn to sleep upon the ground,
> March in your armour thorough watery fens,
> Sustain the scorching heat and freezing cold,
> Hunger and thirst, right adjuncts of the war;
> And, after this, to scale a castle wall,

Besiege a fort, to undermine a town,
And make whole cities caper in the air.

The savage splendour of the man seemed to me the perfect complement to the wild grandeur of the region.

To travel across Asia in the steps of Tamerlane – that was my objective, and it was that ambition which had led me to the state of perilous discomfort I have described. Travelling across the rugged mountain ranges and the arid, dusty plains of Asia has never been a venture to be lightly undertaken nor to be accomplished without suffering. When contemplating my own trip, I had first considered how Tamerlane himself had travelled. It was of little practical assistance to me because he had moved not as a traveller, nor even as a conventional army, but as only a Tartar horde could move: he had moved with everyone and everything that belonged to him. He had campaigned with his massed cavalry squadrons, each man with his spare mount. He had been supported by the many thousands of camels constituting his baggage train. Not only his own harem, but all the women of his army had frequently travelled with the camp. The households of the Emirs and Khans were carried in litters or travelled still in their felt tents (*kibitkas*) which were placed standing on wheeled platforms and dragged by oxen. Lesser wives and concubines rode ponies or camels, carrying with them children and new-born babies. Herds of cattle and flocks of sheep followed the army, grazing in fresh pastures when the terrain was fertile and being themselves slaughtered for food when the going was harder. Sporting accoutrements were not forgotten: many a man carried his falcon on his wrist, and in the households of the richer Khans it was not unusual to see a leopard or cheetah – blindfolded and muzzled – carried across the crupper of a saddle in the hope of finding stags or other game at which they could be set. Many beasts of burden were employed in carrying the siege equipment: ladders, catapults, bombards and excavating machines. Craftsmen brought the tools of their trade; armourers and tailors, butchers and bakers, saddlers and knife-grinders – all were required. On the later campaigns, Tamerlane even took with him his *pièce de résistance*: the twenty-eight war elephants that he had captured on his Indian expedition. When the Tartar horde pitched camp, a veritable township was immediately established in which every man, woman, child and animal had its allotted place. One might aspire to follow in the steps of Tamerlane, but one could not aspire to follow them in the manner of Tamerlane.

So I turned my attention to other travellers who had followed all or some of the same route, to see whether their example proved of any more practical guidance. The first fully recorded traveller to tread in Tamerlane's steps was a fellow diplomat – the illustrious Ruy Gonzales Clavijo, chamberlain of King Henry III of Castile, who was sent as an ambassador to Tamerlane. Clavijo had sailed from Cadiz to Constantinople where, after one false attempt in which he was shipwrecked and narrowly escaped with his life and treasure, he had eventually taken ship through the Bosporus and across the Black Sea to Trebizond.

It was from Trebizond that Clavijo set out on his serious overland journey, accompanied by two companions – a captain in the Castilian royal guard, and a priest – and a retinue comprising various servants and horses. Though not subjected explicitly to violent robbery, they were waylaid by robber barons along their route who pointed out to them the difficulty of earning a living in those parts except by the expedient of requesting presents from those rich travellers who happened to place themselves under their protection. When he came within the domain of Tamerlane, his immunity from assault and robbery improved; but his danger of collapse from exhaustion increased, because Tamerlane sent a series of officials to meet and escort him, each of whom was more assiduous than his predecessor in hastening the ambassador to the monarch's presence.

And thus it was that a frantic race across Persia and Central Asia ensued: Tamerlane was returning from his camp in the Caucasus to his capital at Samarkand, and Clavijo – having just failed to catch him in camp – never quite caught up with him *en route*. Relays of horses were provided and frequently the weary envoy was obliged to ride by night as well as day; indeed, as the temperature rose and the desert conditions deteriorated, day-time travel was almost too rigorous to endure. One of his companions, the robust Captain of the Guard, collapsed and died. As the pace of travel quickened, so the pace of receiving and giving presents accelerated; the nearer the visitors approached to Samarkand, the more frequently they were presented with gold-embroidered cloaks. The sensible ambassador folded and loaded them carefully on to his baggage train, and them promptly passed them on as his own gifts to the next host. Only in this way did he manage to keep intact the presents he was carrying from King Henry to Tamerlane himself. Sporting falcons were the most valuable of these royal gifts and so coveted were they that many along the route tried to induce Clavijo to part with them. His staunch resistance to hints and outright requests from his hosts along the road was rendered somewhat pointless when the prize falcon followed the Captain of the Guard, dying of heat exhaustion. One thing above all I had learnt from reading Clavijo's account of his journey: never should the Asian traveller run out of suitable gifts for those who befriend, or might be induced to befriend, him along his way.

In the centuries following Tamerlane's epoch, there had been few European travellers in his region. One intrepid Elizabethan merchant adventurer – Anthony Jenkinson – had, however, penetrated to the court of the Shah of Persia. We know less about his journey than about Clavijo's; he travelled through Russia to Bukhara, went on into Persia to deliver valuable gifts and letters from Queen Elizabeth I to the Shah, and returned via the Caspian Sea and the Volga river. A few years later, in 1579, another Englishman – Christopher Burroughs – built a ship on the shores of the Caspian and pursued a fitful trade across that sea. In 1598, two English brothers – Sir Anthony and Robert Shirley – reached Persia, and the younger brother was subsequently sent back by the Shah to act as his ambassador at western courts. In the eighteenth century, English and other European traders periodically penetrated to Persia but seldom to Central Asia: John Elton undertook to build a fleet for Nadir Shah, and Jonas Hanway wrote* about his wanderings around Nadir Shah's Persia. But none of these provided much practical guidance for a traveller who wished to retrace the steps of Tamerlane.

The nineteenth-century travellers were only slightly more frequent and marginally more helpful. This was the period of 'the Great Game', of the imperial rivalry between the Russian empire of the Tsars and the Indian empire of the British Raj. Both powers were endeavouring to dominate the emirates of Central Asia and extend their influence over Afghanistan and Persia. The Great Game was a dangerous pursuit for those personally involved in it. The Emir of Bukhara was a particularly unendearing host to those sent to bring him within the pale of

---

* Jonas Hanway's account of his travels in Persia was published *c.* 1750.

British influence: in 1839 he threw the unfortunate Colonel Stoddart (who had disappointed him by bringing no gifts or signed letters from Queen Victoria) into his infamous Black Well, a twenty-foot pit seething with reptiles and vermin specially bred by the sadistic Emir the better to torment his prisoners. Although eventually released from the pit, Stoddart was held at Bukhara, where he was joined five years later by Captain Conolly of the Bengal Light Cavalry, who had come to rescue Stoddart but who – with singular lack of foresight – was also inadequately provided with credentials and tokens of esteem for the Emir, and thus became a second hostage. As the British expeditions against Afghanistan suffered setbacks, so the treatment of the British representatives in Bukhara deteriorated. Eventually reports filtered out of Central Asia to the effect that the two officers had been executed. At this juncture, an eccentric but indefatigable Church of England clergyman, Dr Joseph Wolff, raised a fund and set off single-handed to discover their fate. Here was a traveller who would surely have much wisdom to impart.

Wolff took a route almost identical to that of Ambassador Clavijo five centuries before. He sailed to Constantinople, arriving there in November 1843, and was entertained by Sir Stratford Canning (the British Ambassador) and his wife. They were concerned at his inadequate equipment for the trek that lay ahead of him, and Lady Canning 'bought him flannels so that he should not catch cold'. She also provided him with tea, sugar, a saddle and bridle, and – even more thoughtfully – had various letters of introduction from the Sultan of Turkey to the Emir of Bukhara sewn into the lining of his clerical coat. Indeed, almost the only provisions with which Wolff seems to have thought of providing himself were 'an ample supply of Bibles and Testaments' and 'two or three dozen silver watches';

with these he intended to smooth his path among a population of rapacious infidels whose interest in the latter category of wares was likely to be considerably greater than in the former.

Thus provisioned, and wearing his gown, hood and shovel hat, Dr Wolff sailed across the Caspian to Trebizond, whence he set out over the mountains of Erzurum. He was accompanied by a Serbian servant, a Tartar guide and a Turkish attendant who walked beside his horse uttering reassuring cries when their path approached uncomfortably close to any precipice. A week's travel brought them to the fortified citadel of Erzurum. Here he spent Christmas as the weather deteriorated and the passes became progressively snowbound. Even Lady Canning's flannels were inadequate protection against the weather and he acquired 'a large, loose coat, entirely lined with fur of wolf's skin and large leather boots like the Horseguards that come up to my hips . . . attached to the fur coat was a fur hood to draw over my fur cap . . . I was a Wolff in wolf's clothing.' So clad he skirted the snow-covered flanks of Mount Ararat and pressed on over the Armenian mountains into Persia, having less than friendly encounters with Kurdish tribesmen, until he reached Tabrīz. From there he rode on to Tehrān, where he forcefully explained his mission to the Shah and collected further letters of commendation (despite his tendency to interrupt His Imperial Majesty in mid-sentence), and then pressed on to Mashhad.

The eastern Persian province of Khorāsān had unhappy memories for Wolff because it was there – on a previous missionary expedition – that he had been captured by a robber chieftain, stripped of his clothes, tied to a horse's tail and offered for sale as a slave 'for the unflattering price of £2.10s.' This time his crossing of Khorāsān was less eventful and he was given a further escort of 'nine rascals of the Marwee tribe' to protect him on the remainder of his way across the Turkoman territory; to ensure the good behaviour of the Marwee, the governor of Mashhad threatened that if they proved troublesome (which they did) he would 'burn their wives and children who remain in my hands'.

The final stages of his journey, across inhospitable desert infested by rapacious tribesmen who frequently were in possession of the only wells, were enlivened by conversation with a caravan of merchants from Bukhara and Samarkand who, according to Wolff, 'told stories of Tamerlane as if he were still alive'. When eventually he reached Bukhara, having shed his wolf fur and wearing full canonicals to impress the Emir and inhabitants, he found that Stoddart and Conolly were already dead; he had three uncomfortable months there before he himself could obtain his release. I pondered the remarkable tale. The experiences of Stoddart, Conolly and Wolff might seem remote to the point of irrelevance, but one lesson stuck in my mind: letters of introduction (or the absence of them) seemed to play a disproportionate role in Central Asia.

In the 1870s, another Englishman of a very different character – Captain Fred Burnaby – travelled extensively and adventurously over this area by horse. On one trip he rode right across Asia Minor from Constantinople to Khvoy in Persia, accompanied only by his English soldier servant and by a Turk whose services he acquired *en route* together with those of 'a stud' of five horses. Captain Burnaby's trip coincided with the Turkish preparations for a Russian invasion: everywhere he went he inspected military defences and commented on their inadequacy. His own personal defences, however, were of a very elaborate nature: he himself carried an express rifle, a 12-bore shot-gun and a pistol; and he issued his entourage with 'short travelling swords' and other weapons. His cartridges

were 'mixed up with medicine bottles' to elude detection at
frontiers. I knew that parts of the region through which I
wished to travel still had a reputation for lawlessness, but saw
no prospect of being able to make my journey with an armoury
such as Captain Burnaby had transported.

One traveller who had been determined to see Central Asia
in comfort was that 'very superior person – George Nathaniel
Curzon'. Although he visited the region only forty-five years
after Wolff (in 1888) it was already a different world. The Trans-
caspian Railway had just been opened, so when the Hon. George
Curzon M.P. crossed to the eastern shores of the Caspian he
was able thereafter to traverse the deserts, which had nearly
been the undoing of so many earlier travellers, in the comparatively luxurious comfort of an imperial Russian train. Everywhere there was evidence of Russian control and security: a
regiment of Cossacks was stationed at Merv, and former
Turkoman rebels were proudly decked out in Tsarist uniforms.
What could this sybarite traveller contribute to my own ideas
of how to plan a trip? Perhaps one piece of equipment which
he took should have given me food for thought – an inflatable
rubber bath.

There have of course been other and more recent travellers
to penetrate the spirit as well as the locality of Tamerlane's
world. In the early 1930s, Robert Byron and Christopher
Sykes made a memorable journey through Persia and Afghanistan, recorded in *Road to Oxiana* – a lively hotchpotch of
sensitive observations, informed architectural criticism, and
practical advice about coping with crotchety officials and mud-
swamped roads. Byron's book is a delightful introduction to
Timurid civilization, to the monuments which Tamerlane's
successors left behind them in the lands which he had conquered
for them. It contains terrible warnings against the hazards of

falling sick or hiring cars, or joining unknown companions or disguising oneself as a Persian.

A few years later, in 1938, another Englishman (or rather, Scotsman) was to impinge on Tamerlane's country from the Soviet Union. Sir Fitzroy Maclean, then a young diplomat at the British Embassy in Moscow, was arrested at gunpoint as he penetrated the plains of Qarabagh where Tamerlane had so often camped and hunted tiger in the long grass. Later he managed to reach Bukhara, almost as inaccessible in Stalin's Russia as in the Emir's heyday, and cross the Oxus into Afghanistan. Sometimes his credentials got him out of trouble; more often his own distinctive mixture of charm, persistence and ingenuity accounted for his progress through forbidden regions.

All these travellers had managed to get close to the land and people that intrigued me. They had inspired me to make my own ventures into the region when I, in turn, had been a very young diplomat at the Moscow Embassy. I had traversed the Caucasus by the Georgian Military Highway and ended up in Persia; I had travelled six days on a train to Samarkand and had made my own crossing of the Oxus into Afghanistan.

Now I was determined to embark on a more thorough exploration of Tamerlane's domain. The question was how. From reading the accounts of these earlier travellers I had learnt something of the hazards of journeying the hard way across this tract of Asia; and there was no easy way to follow the route of Tamerlane. He had not kept to those natural highways which had now been transformed into railway lines or trunk roads: he had forced mountain passes or braved desert crossings. I began to contemplate how I could best follow his path. If I were to drive, even by Land Rover, there would be sections of the route I could not follow. And in any case, the occupant of a motor vehicle is largely divorced from the life of the country through which he passes. But if I were to retrace a whole campaign by horse, let alone by mule or on foot, it might take me several years; Tamerlane himself had taken three years on one campaign and five on another. The answer seemed to be to travel by local transport where this existed on the route, and by whatever horse, camel, pony or mule could be found where more mechanized transport could not contend with the rigours of the terrain.

Having considered how to make my journey, the next question was whether to make it alone or with a companion. I was not left to cogitate long about this. My wife, Caroline, had for some time been noticing a growing pile of books about Tamerlane and maps of Iran and Turkey infiltrating the house. Her suspicions that something was afoot were aroused.

'By the way,' she said cheerfully at breakfast one morning, 'I saw a copy of your book about the Andes on our host's book-shelf after dinner last night, and he said he thought the dedication was charming.'

'It was to you, wasn't it?'

'I know it was, darling, but it was the actual wording he thought was so sweet.'

My intellectual antennae are never their most sensitive at breakfast, but even so I sensed the conversation was not as idle as it appeared. How exactly had I worded that dedication? It all came back to me – 'To Caroline, who says she wants to come too next time.' She interrupted my train of thought.

'Were you planning another little trip soon, darling? I was just thinking . . .'

'Yes?'

'I was just thinking that you really will need a proper photographer next time you write a book about a journey. And although I haven't quite finished that course at the Institute, they did say . . .'

'Are you trying to tell me something?' I asked rather unhelpfully.

By the end of breakfast, Caroline was a founder member of the expedition.

Though 'expedition' is perhaps the wrong word. Expeditions sound so solemn and professional. If my journey were to be a proper expedition, it would have to acquire an approved – and preferably scientific – purpose; I should feel obliged to look for sponsors, to set myself specific objectives, to approach the whole undertaking in an earnest frame of mind. Also, I remembered some good advice from a fellow diplomat: 'Never call yourself an expedition,' he said. 'It just invites the local authorities to demand special passes and permissions for everything you want to do. Far better go as a tourist.'

But 'tourist' too had its snags. While it is true that tourist flights, tourist packages and tourist excursions tend to be cheaper than ordinary rates, none of these economical devices ever get very far off the beaten track; certainly, I felt, they would not get me on to Tamerlane's track over the plains and mountains. No: I did not intend to set myself up as an explorer on an expedition, nor as a tourist on an excursion. I was – purely but far from simply – a traveller.

But by what route was I to travel if I was to find the heart of my region and to emulate my chosen predecessor? Tamerlane had campaigned frequently and extensively over great tracts of Russia, Afghanistan, Iran, Turkey, Iraq, Pakistan and India, and over a score of emirates now absorbed into one or other of these countries. Which route was I to choose; which campaign was I to follow? I turned to the accounts of Tamerlane's career

A reconstruction of Tamerlane's head from the
skull excavated by Gerasimov in 1941

The mausoleum of the Mongol ruler Oljeitu at Soltānīyeh

to try to find a single journey which both had been important to him and would cover the area of greatest interest to me. To achieve my purpose I had to look more closely at Tamerlane's whole life story; few more curious ones have ever been recorded.

C

Chapter 2

The Scourge of God

At first sight there is something singularly inappropriate about the fact that 1336, the year in which Tamerlane was born, was the Year of the Mouse in the Mongol calendar. But when the old Kirgiz legend about the naming of the years is recalled, the inappropriateness is less certain. The calendar is a twelve-year cycle, and the story is that the animals lined up to have the years named after them. The camel, being reputed the noblest, took precedence even before the tiger, the dragon and the horse, and far before the dog and the pig. But the mouse, fearing it was so insignificant that no year at all would be named after it, crept up on the camel's neck and along its nose, so that when the procession passed the mouse was in front of all the other animals and the first year of the cycle was named after it. Such craftiness was not uncharacteristic of the young Tartar born onth e ninth of April 1336. The baby was said – by local tradition – to have been born with blood in the palms of his hands: a sure sign that he would slay many men.

Timur (for he cannot yet properly be referred to as Timur-the-lame or Tamerlane) was the son of a minor chief of the Barlas clan, who were Mongols settled in Mawarannhr – that part of the former empire of Genghis Khan which lay in the region subsequently to become known as Transoxiana and which is now the Soviet Socialist Republics of Turkmenistan and Uzbekistan (within the Soviet Union). The main settlements of the region were at Samarkand and Bukhara, but Timur's family came from the little inhabited Qashka-Darya valley. His family, though well-connected, were not (as has sometimes been claimed) directly descended from Genghis Khan; however, medieval genealogists managed to trace both Timur and Genghis back to a maiden named Alan-Goa, whose existence is not made any the more convincing by reports that she was ravished by a moonbeam.

However exotic his ancestry may have been, Timur's childhood is likely to have been earthy enough. He never learnt to read or write, but he early acquired a mastery of both the Turkic and Persian languages. While many of the Mongol descendants who had settled on the Qashka-Darya were farmers in the valleys, Timur's own family appear always to have been warrior nomads. The emphasis in his upbringing was undoubtedly on horsemanship, archery and hunting. At all of these he excelled. From an early age he led his own band of foragers, raiding caravans and stealing cattle from more prosperous or vulnerable neighbours.

It is from this stage of his life that one of the earliest tales of his prowess originates. Timur's band had been scouring the countryside in search of booty and trouble when a larger band of horsemen approached them and made as if to join battle. Timur rode out to challenge their leader in single combat and as his opponent charged down on him – sabre in hand – Timur recognized his war-cry as that of the Barlas. Too late to withdraw, Timur saw that his adversary was his own father. He snatched with his hand at the sabre menacing him, and arrested its descent at the cost of nearly severing his own fingers from his hand. A *rapprochement* ensued. This tale had generally been treated as apocryphal until Dr Gerasimov, the Soviet archaeologist who excavated Timur's tomb in 1941, confirmed injuries to Timur's hand which could only have been inflicted by a savage cut from the inside.

Two cycles of the Mongol calendar had gone by before, in 1360 – another Year of the Mouse – the name of Timur first made its appearance in the chronicles of history as opposed to legend. The Jats of Moghulistan, another branch of the Mongol descendants who had settled in the region north of Mawarannhr, invaded the home country of the Barlas clan in that year. Timur, who was already a formidable figure in the Qashka-Darya valley, did not resist the invaders, but accepted from their hands the governorship of the region. He further consolidated his position by taking as his wife the sister of Emir Husayn, ruler of the neighbouring region of Balkh on the frontiers of what is now Afghanistan. He and Husayn soon broke with their Jat masters, however, and took to the life of roving rebels. Their adventures together in the mountains and deserts were legion: hunger, thirst, imprisonment and wounds were their repeated experience. It was from this period that Timur's lameness stems: an arrow through the right leg during a skirmish in Khorāsān accounted for his nickname of Timur-i-lenk – Timur the lame or Tamerlane. (It is characteristic of Tamerlane that when later in life he caught up with his assailant, he had him strung up and shot to death with arrows: Tamerlane was never to be a forgiving man.)

So successful were these exploits of Tamerlane and Husayn that eventually the Jats were obliged to withdraw from Transoxiana; the former rebels rode in triumph into Samarkand, and Tamerlane had his first experience of being a conqueror. It was not to last for long. The Jats attacked again in 1365 and a memorable engagement ensued, generally known as the Battle of the Mire because torrential rainfall turned the battleground into a quagmire in which horses and men floundered in mud and blood for two days of bitter fighting. The seeds of the breach between Tamerlane and Husayn were sown in this encounter, when Husayn refused to respond to Tamerlane's urgings to advance at a crucial moment in the battle. Eventually Tamerlane and Husayn were forced to withdraw, leaving 10,000 of their warriors dead in the mire and the road open for a Jat advance on Samarkand.

The city of Samarkand saved itself by its own exertions. The citizens under their Sarbadars – self-appointed leaders – resisted the Jats until such time as disease had spread through the horses of the Jat cavalry, forcing the latter to abandon the siege. The Sarbadars then established their own government in the city, but Tamerlane and Husayn still considered Samarkand to belong to them. They returned and invited the Sarbadars to a conference at their camp in the beautiful Meadow of Roses outside the city. No sooner did the Sarbadars arrive at the rendezvous than they were summarily accused of hideous crimes and promptly hanged. The keeping of good faith was never to be a notable characteristic of Tamerlane.

Tamerlane's only rival to power in Samarkand was now his companion in arms and brother-in-law, the Emir Husayn. Indeed, Husayn was the senior of the two and the taxes which he imposed fell heavily on Tamerlane's Barlas people. Knowing this, Tamerlane now displayed that characteristic munificence which was to lend lustre to his name throughout his career. He paid off his kinsmen's taxes from his own purse, even sacrificing his wife's jewellery to the purpose. The contrast between this openhandedness with all that was his to give, and Husayn's grasping acceptance of his own sister's jewels in payment of dues, did not escape the people of Samarkand. There was now little love lost between the two leaders.

Indeed, for the next few years, until 1370, Tamerlane divided his energies between fighting the Jats and fighting his former associate Husayn. His contest with the latter ebbed and flowed along the valleys of Transoxiana, but eventually Husayn established himself at Balkh – the centre of his home country – while Tamerlane consolidated his grip of the regions around Samarkand, winning the support not only of the nomad tribes but also of the craftsmen in the towns and even of those pillars of the Muslim faith, the mullahs. Eventually a trial of strength was inevitable. Tamerlane marched on Balkh, taking his army through the dramatic defile in the mountains – known as the Iron Gate – which protected his homelands for so long from invasion from the south. The assault on Balkh was savagely pressed home. One contemporary authority, Nizam al-din Shami, described how 'famous heads rolled in the streets as numerous as balls in a polo game' (a strange analogy unless the game of polo – already well-established in Persia – had very different rules then from now). The city fell and Husayn sought refuge in the minaret of a nearby mosque, being unluckily surprised there by one of Tamerlane's soldiers who had climbed the minaret to spy out the whereabouts of a runaway horse. Tamerlane had promised earlier in the fighting that if Husayn surrendered his life would be spared. Now his old comrade and rival was brought a prisoner before him. Tamerlane was reminded of his promise and did not order the execution of Husayn; on the other hand, he did not intervene to prevent one of his chiefs who had a grudge against Husayn from murdering him in cold blood, nor did he subsequently intervene to prevent Husayn's kinsmen from murdering the chief in question. Already it was discernible that those who came be-

tween Tamerlane and the sunshine did not long survive to en-
joy their temerity. Husayn's sons were burnt alive and their
ashes scattered.

No sooner was Husayn dead than Tamerlane appropriated
four of his wives to himself. These included a princess descended from Genghis Khan and, through her, Tamerlane
acquired the title of 'Gurgan', or son-in-law of the Great Khan.
Tamerlane was now in reality and in name the ruler of southern
Mawarannhr; he was enthroned in state, a golden crown was
placed (by himself – like Napoleon) on his head, precious stones
were poured over him and he was hailed as 'Conqueror of all
the World'. This he was not yet: but he had set his mind to
it.

His next objectives were to complete his sway over the
neighbouring regions of Moghulistan (to the north-east of
Samarkand towards Lake Balkash) and Khwarazm (to the
north-west towards the Aral Sea). He campaigned in these
directions throughout the 1370s, sacking recalcitrant towns and
fortresses, sending back slaves and craftsmen to Samarkand,
and furthering his own reputation for courage, brutality and
munificence. He accepted a challenge from the Emir of
Urgench to meet him in single combat, only to find that the
prudent emir retracted his challenge. Tamerlane responded by
sending him fresh melons in a golden dish: a lordly gesture
made the more impressive by the niggardly response of the
emir, who rejected the melons and kept the dish. The
repute of Tamerlane was spreading even faster than his
conquests.

The next great project was the conquest of the kingdom of
Hulagu. Named after a grandson of Genghis Khan, this territory comprised western Afghanistan, the whole of Persia, the
fertile valleys of the Tigris and Euphrates in Mesopotamia, and

Armenia; but this formerly cohesive kingdom had fallen into decay, and Tamerlane calculated that it was ripe for intervention. He knew the riches of Khorāsān (eastern Persia) from his early marauding adventures there with Husayn, and he resolved to subjugate this part of the kingdom first. The centre of all the trade passing through Khorāsān was Herat. It was at this staging post, on a variant of the old Silk Road, that goods from the Mediterranean mingled with wares from Central Asia: brocades, spices, rubies, lapis lazuli, camels, Circassian slaves, silver daggers, honey . . . all were to be had in the markets of Herat. In 1381, Tamerlane besieged this rich prize and its Prince surrendered the city to him; Tamerlane sent all movable treasure home (including much that can hardly have been expected to prove movable, such as the huge wrought-iron gates of the city, which were dispatched to adorn the conqueror's birthplace), demolished the town walls, and imposed heavy taxes on the citizens. Two years later, the same citizens of Herat made the grave error of rebelling against Tamerlane's rule. The revolt was quickly put down, and a tower built with the skulls of the culprits.

Now other towns further west – Neyshābūr, Sabzevār and later Soltānīyeh – put themselves under Tamerlane's protection. But on the steep, wooded slopes of the Elburz mountains along the southern shores of the Caspian the independent hill peoples held out against Tamerlane and continued to raid the caravan routes. In 1382, while on his way to this troublesome region, Tamerlane encountered one fortress in Khorāsān which felt sufficiently secure within its walls to offer defiance: this was Kalat, near Mashhad. Tamerlane pretended to lift the siege of this stronghold just long enough for its foolish ruler to let all the livestock out of the fortress into the neighbouring pastures in nearby valleys. He then blocked the passes by which the cattle could return, and starved out the defenders of Kalat. At Isfizar, south of Herat, the rebellious citizens were considered to have given the conqueror much trouble and – as a lesson to others – two thousand of the captives were piled alive one on the other and cemented together with clay to form tall towers which could be seen for miles around – and spoken of for hundreds of miles around. From Isfizar, Tamerlane swept south to Zaranj where, in the course of the fighting, Tamerlane had his horse shot under him: as a consequence of this affront, no prisoners were taken, the walls of Zaranj were levelled to the ground and the drifting sands of the desert allowed to erase all traces of the town.

So far, Tamerlane's *modus operandi* had been a series of short campaigns, usually starting from Samarkand and lasting no longer than a single season, to make fresh conquests or to put down trouble which had arisen in the area of former conquests. Now he was to change his whole pattern of campaigning. Two factors conspired to make him do this: one was the emergence of a formidable foe who could not be vanquished in a single season's campaigning, and the other was a growing desire to undertake even more ambitious and far-flung conquests. It was at about this time that one of his chroniclers remarked: 'As there is only one God in heaven, so there should be only one King on earth.'

The foe was Tokhtamish, khan of the Tartar force known as the Golden Horde (so called because of the splendour of their encampment), and the immediate provocation was Tokhtamish's seizure of Tabriz. Not only was Tabriz central to Tamerlane's plan for the conquest of the Hulagid kingdom, but the fact that it had been stormed and sacked by Tokhtamish was particularly upsetting to him, because Tokhtamish was, to some extent, his own protégé. Indeed, when Tokhtamish had been ousted from the leadership of the lesser White Horde in 1376, it was Tamerlane who had sheltered and supported him. And now that Tokhtamish's fortunes had recovered and he had not only resumed the leadership of the White Horde but achieved the leadership of the more powerful Golden Horde too, he had the effrontery to attack Tabrīz at a time (in 1385) when Tamerlane himself was moving towards that very goal.

So it came about that Tamerlane set out in 1386 – the Year of the Tiger – on the most formidable task he had yet set himself: a three-year campaign to drive the Golden Horde away from the fringes of Persia, and to secure that country for himself. He made careful arrangements for the management of his affairs in and around Samarkand, and warned his lieutenants that they must prepare for a long absence from home. Once he had made up his mind to action, Tamerlane never wasted time. Having given out that he was marching to the east, he in fact pressed on by forced marches into Persia – further west than he had ever been before. By the time he reached the approximate longitude of Tehrān, he was inexorably launched on possibly the most remarkable enterprise of his whole remarkable career.

Before he returned home to Samarkand, he was not only to cross the Elburz, relieve Tabrīz, invade the Caucasus and penetrate deep into Armenia; but he was also to sweep back across southern Persia – through Kurdistan and Luristan – to Isfahan, Persepolis and Shīrāz before turning again towards Central Asia. His route was to traverse the very heart of the region which had so fascinated me. The mountain passes and the mighty rivers he had crossed would be unchanged today; the castles and cities he had stormed might well have changed but would not have disappeared.

For me, there was no need to delve further: this campaign alone and in itself embodied the journey I wished to make. Tamerlane's future thrusts towards Moscow, Delhi or China I would leave to others. This, his first test of sustained endurance, would be my model.

Chapter 3

Assassin Castles

'The start of a journey in Persia resembles an algebraical equation: it may or may not come out' wrote Robert Byron; and this was the mood in which we too set out.We started our travels at the point where Tamerlane's campaign started in earnest, that was after several weeks of forced marches had brought him to central Persia – or (as the Tartars preferred to call it after their Mongol ancestor) the Kingdom of Hulagu. From here on, although still well within his own domains, Tamerlane was operating in country where insurrection was intermittent and harassment endemic. He changed his order of march and proceeded from here westwards with a vanguard of mail-armoured warriors, with his Tartar cavalry fanned out on his flanks, and with the baggage animals and women in the centre of his column. Not that he expected trouble until he reached the foothills of the Elburz mountains, which – running between his line of advance and the southern shores of the Caspian Sea – provided a refuge for potential antagonists.

We did not expect difficulty either until that point. Caroline and I embarked on the first, and undoubtedly the easiest, stage of our 3,000 mile journey: we boarded a comfortable, air-conditioned, long-range bus at Tehrān with tickets for Qazvīn, a small town just under a hundred miles to the north-west on the road to Tabrīz. We sat back and enjoyed watching the Persian landscape unroll, like a series of framed miniatures, outside the window.

Qazvīn, when we reached it, was not what we had expected. In the 1960s, Sir Roger Stevens had found it a slumbering, old-fashioned town with 'life running on amid the ruins and grinding gradually to a stop'. It appeared to have gained a fresh lease of life in the 1970s. Although it was already dark when we arrived, there was bustle everywhere. The main street is flanked with unexciting two-storey houses, but between these are gaps with narrow alleys or precipitous flights of worn and perilous steps. Through these gaps one glimpses half-lit scenes of timeless activity: cauldrons are being boiled, sheep are being slaughtered, children are crouching watchfully.

Iranians eat out little in the provinces. We had patrolled the high street twice before finding a minute establishment serving shashlik, where three or four rather grubby tables were occupied by cheerful soldiery. We were directed up a rickety stair to a little balcony room where skewers of meat and glasses of tea were brought to us. Nothing else was available, and still being hungry afterwards, we went on to an icecream bar; here again it was indicated that Caroline would prove an intolerable distraction to the all-male company, and we were firmly shown upstairs. There we found an Iranian girl seated at a table with two men, breast-feeding her baby. The social conventions of the East have a pattern which defies Western logic.

Our hotel in Qazvīn was neither good nor cheap, but we slept well enough despite a nocturnal call to the faithful from a nearby minaret. In the morning we set out to see what remained in Qazvīn of the town which Tamerlane would have taken in his stride as he marched westward in the spring of 1386.

The one place he would have been certain to have visited was the Friday Mosque, the main congregational mosque of the town. The sanctuary is a massive construction dating from the Seljuk dynasty who ruled this part of Persia from A.D. 1037 until the Mongol invasion of 1220. But like most ancient mosques, the Friday Mosque of Qazvīn has been overlaid with constructions of many later styles. To reach the Seljuk heart of the mosque we passed first through a magnificent and decorative gateway built by Shah Ismail at the beginning of the sixteenth century, and then passed down a long passage which ended in a grille of blue tiles. Beyond we could see tantalizing glimpses of domes and minarets. To left and to right narrower passages delved through the masonry to emerge in a quadrangle of impressive proportions, studded with plane trees and carpeted with a mosaic of old brick and tufts of unkempt grass. The morning light played gently on the *iwans* – the domed portals set into the side walls of the mosque, the largest of which as always faced towards Mecca. It was here, beyond the south *iwan*, that we could identify the solid, heavy Seljuk building in which Tamerlane doubtless prayed for the success of his forthcoming campaign.

We sat on the edge of an ornamental pond and watched the cats play among the crumbling masonry, and wondered whether Tamerlane had found more satisfaction here than in the portable wooden mosque that he carried (like some ark of the covenant) on his campaigns with him. No other human disturbed the peace of this Islamic courtyard possessing the calm and spaciousness of a Cambridge college. We would have been happy to have spent some time there in contemplation, but wilder scenes were calling.

While Tamerlane was worshipping in these mosques at Qazvīn, he had anxieties about his further progress. He was very conscious that the further he travelled westwards, the more vulnerable would become his lines of communication through Qazvīn. Tamerlane was not a man to take chances over his communications at any time, and he was particularly disinclined to leave perils in his rear so close to Soltānīyeh where – as we shall see – he intended to leave the ladies of his harem. The main threat to the road that has run for centuries through Tehrān, Qazvīn and Soltānīyeh to Tabrīz is the proximity to the north of the Elburz mountains. Rising to heights of over 15,000 feet, these are not just an ordinary area of brigand-infested highlands: the folds of these hills contain the dreaded and beautiful Valley of the Assassins.

The sect of the Assassins was founded by Hasan-i-Sabbah at the end of the eleventh century. He was a Shi'a Muslim who had been converted to the Ismaili doctrine before developing his own theological/political philosophy and founding his own sect. The practice of this sect, of which he became the first grand master, was to give a new word to the world: assassination. His enemies were the Seljuk rulers of Persia and the Caliphs of Baghdad. Rather than fight them as a whole, he saw the key to their destruction in the elimination of their leaders. He resolved to allow neither compunction nor sentiment to stand in his way, and his first victim was a former friend and fellow pupil (they had both been at school with Omar Khayyám) called Nizam. This unhappy man had become a Seljuk grand vizier; the followers of Hasan-i-Sabbah cut him down in 1092. Nizam was the first of a long line of distinguished victims who were to leave a trail of blood – shed in the cold of the night rather than the heat of battle – down nearly two centuries and across the whole Muslim world.

Hasan-i-Sabbah set up his headquarters at the Rock of Alamut – 'the eagle's nest' – in the Elburz. There are various theories about how he persuaded his followers to risk – and usually lose – their lives on missions to murder his enemies. The most popular belief is that he chose young men from his sect and had them brought under the influence of drugs to one of the many beautiful groves of the Alamut valley. The entrance to this secret and enchanted valley then lay through a rift in a high wall of rocks. Once within its precincts, the youths would be attended by voluptuous maidens, entertained with music and wine and allowed to bathe in the fresh waters of the valley. They were assured that this was paradise and that, if they obeyed their master's injunctions, even if they were killed in the process, they would return here. They were briefed for their deadly tasks, drugged again and sent from the valley on their missions. Few failed, though many died.

The reputation of the dread Assassins spread throughout Islam. After the death of Hasan-i-Sabbah, they were employed less and less for the quasi-religious motives of their founder and more and more as hired political murderers, working for pay. They were well known to the Christian crusaders, whose revulsion for their methods was tempered with a certain admiration for their discipline and organization. The Seljuks made repeated attempts to penetrate the Alamut valley and destroy their castles, but so impregnable were these that it was not until the Mongol invasion of Hulagu Khan in 1256 that the fortresses were wrested from the Assassins' hands, their reign of terror ended and their valley subjugated. Even then, the Rock of Alamut itself would have held out as it had done before; but the then Master of the Assassins – Rukneddin – had been captured and held hostage by the Mongols, and it was he who ordered the castle to surrender. It profited him little, as the Mongols had him murdered anyway, while he travelled as their prisoner through his own mountain country.

The author and his wife play backgammon,
Tamerlane's favourite game, beside the trail

Old men outside the Cifte Minareli Medrese at Erzurum

The Ark at Tabriz, built by the Mongols

But even a century after these events, it was still an uncomfortable region to have on the flank of a supply line. When Tamerlane had first invaded the former kingdom cf Hulagu he had spent much time in the foothills of the Elburz subduing dissident tribesmen who had been raiding the caravan routes. Such raiding had broken out again. And on this, his most ambitious and longest campaign so far, it was more than ever important that he should not have trouble behind him. The only certain way of ensuring against this was to be more thorough than last time: to send a detachment of his horde up the Alamut valley, across the passes of the Elburz and into the turbulent jungles of the Caspian coast. Only after such a diversion could he turn his back on the Elburz and the Caspian with an easy mind.

We decided that if it was necessary for Tamerlane, it was necessary for us too. To cross the Elburz we would have to find guides and hire mules. None of this could be done in Qazvīn. Our next step was to reach Alamut and the entrance to the Valley of the Assassins. We were told there was one mini-bus a day from Qazvīn to Alamut; but there were differing theories on when and where it left. Eventually we had to scramble aboard with no time to buy any iron rations for the journey that lay ahead of us. It nearly proved a fatal mistake.

The bus set off at a cracking pace across the plain that led to the foothills of the Elburz. Once into the foothills however, the gradient quickly became sharper and the bus lurched uneasily over the rough track and uncomfortably close to cliff edges. We left vegetation behind us and with it our self-confidence.

It suddenly occurred to us that we were setting off to an unknown destination in an area with a notorious reputation for inhospitality; we had virtually no rations or knowledge of the language; we could not carry our own baggage for more than the shortest distance unaided; we did not know where, how, or for how much mules could be hired; and we had all too few *rials*, owing to an inability ever to encounter banks during opening hours.

'Don't worry about the money,' said Caroline, 'I'm told they cut your throat for a very modest sum in these parts.'

Peter Fleming remarks in his *News from Tartary* that every expedition deserves some stroke of luck along the road. Ours came early. We had scarcely been jolting over the stony, biblical landscape for more than an hour, when a young Iranian, with a fringe of beard around the periphery of a cheerful, open face, made his precarious way up the bus towards us and inquired: 'You are an English?'

I confessed I was. He squatted on a satchel in the corridor of the bus and explained, in rapid succession, that he loved all Englishes, that he especially loved the Queen of England, that he loved speaking English to Englishes, that he was a mathematics student at Qazvīn, that the English were very good at mathematics, that his native village was Gazar Khan, that the inhabitants of Gazar Khan did not know any Englishes which was a pity. It was a breathless but friendly performance which, we felt, had somewhat exhausted both him and his vocabulary.

As the bus and our conversation lurched along their uneasy courses, we slowly realized the extent of our luck. Moghim – for that was the student's name – came from the village half-way up the Valley of the Assassins which we had hoped to make our starting point for a crossing of the Elburz. He intended to walk from the point where the road ended, and where our bus would deposit us at the end of our two-and-a-half-hour journey, to his village. He said it would take him three or four hours. We could come with him if we liked. If we wanted to stay at Gazar Khan, his mother would be happy

to put us up. His family would like to meet Englishes. When
we pointed to the size of our suitcases and our resultant im-
mobility without assistance, he was sure he could borrow a
mule to take them up to Gazar Khan. Nothing seemed too
much of a problem to this returning prodigal son.

Our bus finally juddered to a halt at a tiny wooden hut
perched on the side of a hill above a cluster of the dwellings in
the valley below. The wooden hut turned out to be a tea-house.
Inside was a raised wooden platform on which sat or squatted
a number of local *habitués*. Some flat cakes of unleavened bread,
a few spring onions, small glasses of tea and a bowl of sugar
lumps were spread on a plastic cloth in the centre of the
platform. It was lunchtime and we joined them. Moghim sent
small boys scampering down the hillside in search of any
available mules. The minutes and hours passed, measured only
in glasses of tea. More small boys were dispatched to determine
the fate of the earlier ones.

Tea-houses are an institution in Persia. Most travellers have
written affectionately of them, but Professor Browne towards
the end of the last century reported that: 'Many such tea-houses
. . . were closed some time ago by order of the Shah. The
reason commonly alleged for this proceeding is that they were
supposed to encourage extravagance and idleness, or, as I have
also heard said, evils of a more serious kind.' Neither in this
tea-house, nor in any of the many others we were to encounter,
did we find evidence of those dark vices of which the Professor
appears to have been warned.

The hottest part of the day had already passed when we set
out, and the afternoon's walk was idyllic. The mules carried
our cases; the sun was warm but not oppressive; wild flowers
and trilling streams enlivened our path. This was indeed an
enchanted world for which a twelfth-century Persian lad might

well have risked capture, torture and death by fulfilling some murderous mission in a foreign land.

At one point Moghim led us across a high bridge of wooden slats, with no hand-rail, over a fast-flowing stream; the mules were led far downstream to a safe ford and for several miles we pursued different paths up the valley. Later in our travels over more rugged parts of the Elburz we were to be served by more intrepid mules who took such bridges in their stride, as indeed they had to when traversing otherwise uncrossable torrents. But here, in the home valley of the Assassins, life was safer and more leisurely: everyone took his own way in his own time through the sweet-smelling pastures.

It was nearly nightfall as we entered the village of Gazar Khan. The wattle houses nestled among boulders and were interspersed with trees and greenery. Everywhere we picked our way over streams and irrigation channels; rough dust paths joined the houses in a labyrinthine network. We followed Moghim closely and collected behind ourselves a Pied-Piper-like trail of children. The whole village only covered the area of approximately one acre but, owing to the twists and turns of the paths, it seemed as if we had been going for some time before Moghim ducked under a low wattle arch into a diminutive courtyard and was instantly fallen upon by his entire family – mother, brother and little sisters.

He had been away for six months and the welcome was tumultuous. A new goat was led out of its pen under the sleeping quarters and proudly displayed. A new shawl had been woven for the eleven-year-old sister and she flounced round the little mud patch that formed the central courtyard of the house, making flirtatious gestures with it. All was happy excitement and we were caught up in it.

Moghim's mother had a strong, weathered but handsome

face; she had been a widow for many years and bringing up the family had left its mark in the determined set of the mouth and the lines around the eyes. She welcomed us warmly and without surprise, showing us to a small room with mud walls and bright-coloured carpets on the floor. Taking our cue from the pile of shoes on the wooden veranda running round the little courtyard, we took off our boots before going in. The walls were lined with cotton hangings or plastic sheets behind which we could hear the continual rustle of cockroaches and other insects at play. This was Moghim's room, the only one in the house with a table – a simple trestle affair on which Moghim laid out his few mathematics books with obvious pride.

The longest side of the little courtyard formed the kitchen-living-room. Here Moghim's mother and sisters were continually brewing tea or poring over the fire: it was remarkable to us that so much culinary activity could result in so little food. Moghim and his younger brother never went near the kitchen; when they wanted tea or food, they summoned the smallest sister to get her larger sisters to prepare something and bring it to Moghim's room. Men and boys never stirred themselves.

After the first of innumerable small glasses of tea, with lumps of rather unsweet sugar, had been brought to us, as we sat with Moghim and his brother on the floor of his room, Moghim suddenly asked: 'And now, what would you like for dinner?'

It was a difficult question, as we had no idea of what was likely to be available.

'Whatever you usually have,' said Caroline, hesitant and eager not to cause difficulty. Moghim did not understand; his command of the spoken word was greater than his comprehension of the half-listened-to word. Caroline tried repeating what she had said, and then, embarrassed at seeming to ask for something so complicated, changed her ground and said brightly: 'An egg would be lovely.'

The younger brother was dispatched with the order. An hour passed in desultory conversation. Our familiarity with those contemporary English mathematicians whom Moghim professed to admire was minimal (particularly as most of them sounded as if they were in fact German anyway). We took it in turns to wend our way through the livestock in the yard to the pit, shrouded by a broken screen of branches, that constituted the loo. Eventually the brother returned and explained that he had found somewhere where eggs could be bought. Realizing belatedly that we had asked for something beyond the resources of the house, we persuaded Moghim with difficulty that we should be allowed to pay. The emissary was sent forth again, this time with a few coins.

Meanwhile all the activity of the womenfolk in the kitchen had at last brought forth its meagre result. A bowl of rice and a pile of flat sheets of unleavened bread was handed up the stair by Moghim's mother. Some goat cheese and a bowl of *mast*, or yogurt, followed. The women withdrew to the kitchen to eat separately, while we sat around the plastic cloth laid out on the carpet and, remembering to use only our right hands, tore off pieces of bread and scooped up rice with them.

Only when we had already long finished the meal did the eggs appear. They had been lightly fried and allowed to cool on a greasy plate. There were two each for Caroline and me; the family adamantly refused to partake. There were no implements but our fingers.

'Your eggs,' said Moghim with an obvious sense of achievement, passing the dish to Caroline.

'Close your eyes and think of England,' I murmured as Caroline reached out falteringly, deftly folded a slithery egg and popped it in her mouth in a passable imitation of one scooping up the last of the caviare from a silver salver.

'Darling,' she said to me in slow enough English to be understood by Moghim, 'they're *so* delicious I *insist* on your having all the rest.' Caroline can be very generous.

After dinner Moghim and his brother left us, bidding us goodnight and showing us how to extinguish the hurricane lantern when we were ready to sleep. We wrapped ourselves in the pile of blankets left for us and stretched out on the brightly carpeted floor. Not even the scuttling of the cockroaches could keep us awake for long.

We woke early the following morning and peered out in the dawn light into the little courtyard of Moghim's house. His mother and sisters were already stirring, and soon small girls with even smaller glasses of hot tea were being dispatched in our direction. Today was the day we were to climb the Rock of Alamut: Hasan-i-Sabbah's castle and the objective of so many expeditions by Seljuk overlords, Mongol conquerors and intrepid adventurers. Moghim had offered to be our guide, and as soon as breakfast was over we set off.

The face of the Rock of Alamut which is visible from the village of Gazar Khan is almost sheer for nearly a thousand feet, but there was alleged to be an easier line of approach on the reverse side. We climbed out of the village, crossed a stream, skirted the southern flank of the Rock and passed a string of mules emerging from a gully, heavily laden with bags of rice from the Caspian shore.

By then we had reached the reverse side of the Rock. Our hearts fell. It looked as if it could defy with impunity not only the assaults of the Seljuks, but the assaults of ourselves as well. Moghim did not share our hesitation; he led us firmly towards what appeared to be a goat track up the rock face. The loose shingle under our feet shifted disconcertingly and cascaded down into the valley below. Our conversation suddenly dried up under the strain of concentration.

We had various brief halts on the ascent, but looking up was depressing and looking down was terrifying. So we did not really rest until we emerged into a huge cave where we felt safer. The cave had an opening at the far end, the size of a large french window; from this we not only overlooked Gazar Khan, but the whole valley up which we had travelled the previous day. It was from this vantage point that Hasan-i-Sabbah would have watched for the return of the young men he had sent out on their deadly missions.

We spent half an hour clambering through tunnels and cavities in the rock and along the narrow buttresses of masonry that linked the different sections of the castle. From below, Alamut appears as a natural rock formation, not as a man-made fortress. Although now that we had climbed up to it we found plenty of traces of the works of man, the original impression remained the correct one: the defenders of Alamut had been to a large extent troglodytes living in a beehive which nature had constructed for them and which they had 'improved' for their own purposes.

Moghim explained that the Rock was as impervious to siege as it was to attack, since it had its own fresh water springs. There were many legends how the water reached the garrison. One such described a tunnel through the rock leading down to the spring below; skins of water were said to have been slung beneath the bellies of goats who were then encouraged to make a rapid ascent, via the tunnels to the garrison above, by the violent expedient of loosing wolves up the tunnels behind them.

Indeed, there are legends about almost every aspect of life on the Rock of Alamut. One of the most bizarre recounted to us by Moghim (and recorded by earlier travellers) is that Hasan-i-Sabbah stored honey – presumably to sustain and give energy to the defenders – in a deep hole in the interior of the Rock. When the first Mongol invaders scaled the castle, long after Hasan's death, one of their leaders was directed down a tunnel ending in the honey well, into which he fell and drowned.

More macabre still is the tale of Hasan's own death. As a prophet and religious leader, he felt that the immortality of his reputation would be irreparably damaged if he died and was buried like any other mortal. He who had caused death to so many others wished to elude a common end himself. When therefore he felt that his last days had come, he retired into his chamber within the castle and told his servants they were not to enter for three days, after which 'they might come in and would find his soul but not his body within'. Hasan then plunged into a bath of vitriol which, before the three days were up, had completely eaten away all trace of his remains; only a black raven – introduced into the chamber by him before his death – remained to be discovered by the startled attendants.

Pondering these grim tales, we began our descent. It was far slower than the ascent: the shale seemed to have become less stable, our ankles less strong, and Caroline's camera less light. But we had little time to rest on our return. We had already confessed to Moghim our ambition of leaving his valley northwards, to cross the Elburz rather than return to the plains from which we had come. For this we needed a serious guide and sturdy transport. Moghim had put the word around the village about our needs. When we got back from the Rock, both guide and transport were awaiting us: there was to be no backsliding.

Chapter 4

Over the Elburz

On our return from the Rock of Alamut, and while awaiting
the arrival of the guide and mule that Moghim had found, we
packed our meagre possessions together. Perhaps at this point
the somewhat eccentric nature of our luggage should be explained. We had not come on this trip intending to carry our
belongings unaided for long distances, and had therefore rejected the idea of packs or haversacks. Where we were to be
off the beaten track, we envisaged having animals – be they
mules, horses or camels – to take the load. On the other hand,
we knew we should be required to hump our cases over short
distances – in towns, across frontiers and so on. So I had selected
one medium-sized suitcase, and Caroline one medium-sized
grip-bag; they were known to us as the 'pseudo-Guccis', as
both had the distinctive Gucci coloured bands, but neither had
any close connection with that eminent designer.

We had packed books; film and camera tripod (never used);
a few tidy clothes; sleeping bags made of sewn-up sheets, so
that at least we could cocoon ourselves in clean linen however
dirty the bedding we might encounter; a change of shoes; a
light torch; sponge bags, with an additional one full of medica-
ments and suncream; warm sweaters and anoraks (vital on

occasion but an awful bore for ninety per cent of the time); and some gifts (of which more anon). All this left little room for iron rations, which consisted solely of a few oranges and some packets of ginger-nut biscuits. We were not exactly equipped for exploration or mountaineering.

The guide appeared, leading a plump and healthy-looking mule, just as we were completing the ritual of fastening the cases. Could he have his fee now, he asked, as he had some bills to settle before he set off? We reminded him we had agreed to pay him half now, and half on arrival at Shahsāvar – our destin-ation the other side of the Elburz on the Caspian coast. Violent shaking of the head, and a voluble stream of protest, suggested that this was no longer acceptable. I stood my ground. Moghim, torn between good-hostmanship and village solidarity, effected a volte-face and declared I ought to pay the whole sum now. I still stood my ground. Everything I had ever read, heard or learnt by experience suggested that to hand over all one's promised rewards before the outset of a venture was to invite being let down. I was convinced it was a try-on.

'The mule is tired of waiting and is going home,' announced Moghim.

'Let him go,' I said, 'we will find another.' And – much to my surprise and chagrin – he went, led away by his sulky muleteer.

Finding a replacement was not so easy. Moghim's co-opera-tion was diminishing. Eventually, a positively geriatric-looking muleteer with a spindly-looking donkey was produced. He would lead us to Shahsāvar and his donkey would carry our bags. But he declared that the Salambar pass (the route taken by Freya Stark and subsequent travellers) was too windy and too snowy; it would be necessary to go a longer way round further to the west and join the Salambar valley on the other side of the pass.

We were uneasy. I had reservations about the guide, and Caroline said she thought the RSPCA's flying squad would be after us if we so much as placed a roll of film on the ageing donkey. But we sensed that our welcome in Gazar Khan was waning, and it seemed time to thank our host and move on. We fixed a price with the muleteer and he strapped the pseudo-Guccis on the forlorn donkey. Its knees knocking ominously together it set off, the three of us walking behind it into the enveloping mountains.

Geriatric-looking he might be, but our muleteer was no laggard. He set off at a sprightly pace which kept Caroline and me panting in his wake. And he maintained the pace unflaggingly despite the mounting gradient. We passed behind the castle of Hasan-i-Sabbah and soon left the green and pleasant Valley of the Assassins for good. Now we were traversing bare, rocky mountainside which had an almost lunar bleakness.

In a fold in the mountains we saw a tiny hamlet far below us. It took us half an hour to wind our way down to it. We were offered a glass of tea in a wood and wattle hut by a kindly family whose baby, lying in what appeared to be a wicker dog basket, had no legs. They fed and cherished it lovingly, but I wondered about its future: life was hard here for the able-bodied, for the maimed it seemed likely to be either short or intolerable.

All too soon we pressed on. For several hours we saw no further sign of human habitation; and, to increase our discomfort, a sudden hail-storm rattled down on the bleak slopes, leaving us wet through and weary. We would have welcomed a brief rest, but our muleteer's pace never slackened. I was reminded of Freya Stark's conclusion that 'a Persian guide does not look on his employer as a human being: he, like any other registered packet, is an object to be delivered safe at the other end: when and how, the guide considers his own affair'.

Soon we were stumbling over rocks in the half-dark and at times we lost sight altogether of our muleteer and our luggage. It was not only the risk of loss that concerned us about the baggage: there was an additional worry. The language barrier between us and our muleteer was almost total, and we suspected that he thought that our bags contained much more useful materials than was in fact the case. We feared that at any moment he might declare that we had 'arrived' and look to us to produce tents, warm sleeping bags, food and drink. What other contents, we asked ourselves, could he possibly imagine justified the trouble of taking such suitcases with us?

But as we trudged on we derived some comfort from the thought that he would surely have halted by now had he not got a firm objective, in the form of a roof, in mind. And just when we were on the point of despair, we identified the outline of a roof against the rocks below us. The hut at which we arrived was one of a cluster almost at the bottom of a valley encasing a rapidly flowing stream.

Our reception was one of the least welcoming events I can ever remember. Footsore and weary, we had expected to be greeted as guests deserving some consideration; instead of which, we were met by a scowling figure who led us through a pitch-dark passage into a small room illuminated by a flickering lantern. It was crowded: dark, suspicious faces loomed out of the shadows and peered – hostile and greedy – at the new arrivals.

Tired as we were, we felt this was no moment to forget our manners. Painfully we took off our boots at the dusty door, wondering if we should ever find them again in the dense darkness, and stepped over the threshold to join the sinister group within. We saw our luggage being spirited away into even profounder darkness.

We were grudgingly invited to join the circle and collapsed with relief on a rug. Our eyes were now becoming accustomed to the dark, and we could discern new and smaller faces – wide-eyed and less sinister – as various children tiptoed in to join the group and gape in wonder at the curious strangers who had arrived in their midst. Our muleteer was explaining us to the company at large; he himself knew so little about us and our intentions that we wondered what he could be telling them. From time to time we picked out the name Shahsāvar – our hoped-for destination – and we feebly echoed this with enthusiastic smiles. We envied Freya Stark her ability to bandy compliments endlessly on such occasions.

Eventually, after what seemed like an eternity of unintelligible talk, rustlings around the doorway proclaimed the arrival of the traditional glasses of tea. Next came the spreading of a large plastic sheet, and after much coming and going by the women, a pile of unleavened bread, a bundle of green shoots looking and tasting like chives, and several bowls of *mast* were placed in the centre. We were invited to help ourselves.

Our muleteer was my neighbour on the carpet at dinner. It was the first of many meals we were to take in his company, and it was not an agreeable company to be in at mealtimes. His manners were not just rough, they were aggressively greedy. One did not really mind the fact that his mouth remained open while he ate to such an extent that sitting opposite him resembled looking through the porthole of a washing-machine: a succession of ever less recognizable objects rotating in full view. Nor did one really mind the grunts, splutters and gurks that accompanied the process. But one did resent, when we were all equally hungry, the way his grubby hands went out to snatch a morsel of cheese, or the last corner of a sheet of flat bread, from in front of Caroline or his hosts. When offered sugar lumps for his tea, he took a handful; when offered a cigarette by me, he made a grab for three or four.

Our host was tolerant, but not unobservant, of this behaviour. Indeed, the first indications we had that he was not as villainous as he looked were provided by the attention he paid to ensuring that Caroline was not deprived of all means of sustenance by our muleteer: with considerable dexterity he slipped her a bowl of *mast* under the muleteer's armpit as the latter made one of his more far-reaching grabs across the plastic floor-cloth.

In fact, as the meal wore on, our host became almost genial. He had our bags retrieved from whatever dark recesses of his establishment they had been taken to, and placed behind us to lean on, as he could see that we were tired and found sitting cross-legged on the carpet was not the easiest way to rest. He expressed admiration for Caroline's having endured the climb, and paid us compliments on our boots (with no apparent expectation of being presented with them). Then, after much lively conversation with our muleteer, he indicated with gesticulations and many references to Shahsāvar, that he intended to accompany us himself on the morrow. It transpired that he had a relative in Shahsāvar, and also that he could purchase supplies there to bring back. He would take two mules of his own. From that moment onwards, we referred to him between ourselves as the Second Muleteer, and our original companion and guide as the First Muleteer; the echoes of the First and Second Murderers in *Macbeth* did not seem altogether inappropriate.

Indeed, Caroline and I heard the news that we were to be outstrengthed from now on by our companions with mixed feelings. We welcomed any dilution of the First Muleteer's company and the prospect of more baggage animals was welcome to us. But we had no reason to trust our host or his intentions in this wild, desolate and ill-reputed part of the world. The best that could be said for his manner was that it was less hostile than before. We knew we should be completely at his mercy in the lonely mountain passes that lay ahead, and whereas the First Muleteer was at least known to Moghim and our acquaintances in Gazar Khan, the Second Muleteer had no recommendation of any sort to counterbalance his own shifty looks. But there was nothing we could do about it except smile our acquiescence.

One by one the children left the circle, taking the traces of the meal (there was no food left over) with them. One of our host's sons lighted me to a privy between the hut and the stream, and one of the girls did the same for Caroline. Eventually our host indicated a pile of wolf skins, pointed out the smoothest area of the rug-covered floor and bade us goodnight. We were almost too tired to unpack our sheet sleeping-bags, but thought that it might be advisable to insulate ourselves from whatever wild-life inhabited the wolf skins that were to be our bedding. We curled up on the recommended part of the floor while the First Muleteer slept across the doorway, and our dreams were less bizarre than the realities around us.

From early next morning – half an hour before dawn to be precise – we realized that our new companion was in fact to be a substantial asset. To start with, he contributed two strong, healthy mules to our cavalcade. His family had been loading them in the darkness while we slept and, since his main objective was to buy merchandise on the Caspian coast rather than to take goods there, they were not heavily weighed down. Unlike the First Muleteer's unhappy donkey, they were decked

Turkish shepherds in coats made out of sacks

A caravanserai on the road near Bitlis

out with tassels on their bridles and little bells on their tails. They represented a considerable boost to our morale and our transport potential.

The climb out of the gorge in which the Second Muleteer's hut was situated was an exhausting scramble on all fours up an interminable bank of loose scree. An hour after we set out, we were in a state of collapse and still not even out of the gorge. The mules made wide traverses, and even so repeatedly fell on their knees, being ever slower to pick themselves up and re-commence the struggle. Already the tassels looked sadly out of place and the tinkle of the bells seemed a forlorn sound on the great expanse of stony slope.

Eventually we emerged on to more open and less steep terrain. As soon as his animals had got back their wind, the Second Muleteer offered Caroline a ride on one of them. His attentiveness contrasted agreeably with the First Muleteer's persistence in treating us as recalcitrant packages. The sun was now up: not strong enough to melt the surrounding snow, but quite fierce enough to fire our thirst.

It was about midday when we crested yet one more skyline to find, to our delight, that we appeared to have crossed the watershed of the Syalan pass. Ahead of us the way lay more down than up for the first time, and – better still – the bare rock gave way to coarse green grass: there must be water here.

It was the Second Muleteer who spotted the spring. A quarter-mile detour to the east took us to it. We lay on the ground and drank unrestrainedly, in the manner not approved by Gideon when selecting his army to march against the Midianites. The First Muleteer threw stones at the mules to keep them away until we had finished, then they too had their turn.

E

We had imagined when we crossed the watershed that we had no more steep climbs ahead of us; but as the day wore on, we grew weary of confronting fresh ridges. By circumventing the Salambar pass to the west, we had in fact taken a much more arduous route than that chosen by Freya Stark and most later travellers. More than once, we wondered about the First Muleteer's judgement in the choice of pass. Only as evening fell did we see below us the valley of the Seh Hazar river which linked up with the Salambar pass; and to get down to that valley involved some further hours of perilous descent of loose scree. The mules floundered; our own ankles buckled disconcertingly. It was a lame and halting party which reached the first hut we had seen all day.

The following day we started to follow the valley of the Seh Hazar, which we learnt meant 'three thousand', presumably referring to the number of tiny streams and tributaries that flowed into the river. One moment we were perched far above it, our mules walking along the outer edge of the path in the nonchalant way mules do, and the next moment we were winding down to the stream itself, to make a wet-footed crossing of a ford or traverse a rickety wooden bridge with no hand rail.

All the while the vegetation increased in density. Where before we had walked over a carpet of alpine flowers, now we walked beneath mature trees. Conifers gave way to deciduous varieties. Sturdy oaks spread their branches. The stream became a river, carving a wider – though no less steep – cleft through the mountainside.

We travelled in all for twelve hours along the banks of the Seh Hazar. It was one of the most beautiful walks I ever remember anywhere: the continual roar of the river, the shade of the oaks, the overhanging crags of rock, all combined to make this a memorable day – in fact, two days, since we spent a night on the Seh Hazar.

If our recollections of where we slept in the Elburz are shadowy, it is hardly surprising. We almost never saw our shelter in daylight: we arrived as night was fast falling, and we left before the dawn. Our muleteers did not believe in wasting daylight travelling time. But we shall not easily forget the last night of our crossing.

The long, low wooden building where we finally halted was isolated, apart from its own attendant barns. The hut itself was part dwelling and part stable. A raised platform, on which were laid straw mats, ran down the length of the hut, the further extremities of which were lost in darkness. In the centre of the floor burned a large log fire and round it, their faces intermittently illuminated with flashes from the flame, clustered the family – looking like figures from some dark Rembrandt interior. Evelyn Waugh described just such a scene in *When the Going Was Good*: in his case it was a lamp not a fire which 'stood on the floor in the middle of the shelter so that all the faces were illuminated as faces are not meant to be seen; from below with cheek bones casting shadows across their eyes and strong light under the brows, chin and nostrils'.

The people here all looked northwards towards the Caspian for their supplies and contact with the outside world; our own muleteers from the Alamut valley were almost as much strangers as we were ourselves. But otherwise the night followed the pattern of earlier ones in the mountains. We ate the customary meal of *mast*, unleavened bread and goat cheese, and then slept around the open fire in the centre of the floor.

It was too public to undertake any undressing, so Caroline and I lay side by side in the shadows on a pile of rugs and eventually fell asleep to the accompaniment of a soft burble of conversation. I mused as I dozed on the truth of Freya Stark's dictum that 'the capacity for sleeping in public is one of the most useful things one can acquire . . . after a time, the murmur of voices, discussing you over the fire, becomes no more disturbing than the sound of running water to dwellers by a stream'. We had already acquired this capacity. Throughout the night we only stirred as one or other of the sleepers round the fire roused himself sufficiently to put some more wood on the flickering flames.

It was still quite dark when the First Muleteer shook my shoulder far from gently and indicated that we should be on the move. In fact, it was five o'clock and, without even a glass of hot tea, we were on the move at 5.25 a.m. The next two hours saw the river swell out into a less noisy and more dignified waterway; its valley flattened out into a forest of handsome trees; its bridges became sturdier and more serious. Our appreciation of the scenery was, however, modified now by the aches which had developed in almost every limb after several days of hard climbing and hard lying.

And so we were glad when the Second Muleteer indicated that it was time to brew up some tea. We occupied ourselves with boiling the pot and broaching a long-hoarded packet of ginger-nuts – since we now felt that the need to preserve iron rations had passed – while the Second Muleteer collected brushwood and loaded his mules till they looked like Birnam Wood *en route* for Dunsinane. No more would we be offered lifts, but he would be sure of something to sell when he reached the metropolis of Shahsāvar.

The road, when we came to it, was an anticlimax. We had managed well enough on the rough paths and dusty tracks of the Elburz, and now we resented the exposed feeling of the public highway: our little cavalcade had had a dignity in the mountains which it signally lacked as we limped, tattered and tired, along the empty road.

Soon we came to one of the ubiquitous little wooden tea houses, but this one demonstrated its spiritual orientation towards the populated coast in front, rather than towards the bare mountains behind: it displayed a Pepsi Cola sign. We stopped for refreshments and the tea house keeper told us that in an hour or so the daily bus would come and could take us on the final stage of our journey to Shahsāvar. The prospect of not having to walk further on the uninteresting road was a pleasing one, and we decided to wait. But the muleteers announced that they would press on without further delay.

So the moment of parting had come. There was settling up to be done with the First Muleteer, who had fulfilled his contract and earned the residue of his pay. With the Second Muleteer we had no contract; he had chosen to join us for his own reasons. But having done so, he had helped us more assiduously and courteously than our own muleteer. It was he who had given us lifts when we were footsore and weary, and he who had carried Caroline's Nikon tenderly over the crumbling and frightening sections of the path. We could not say farewell and leave him unrewarded. Yet we had a real problem: because of the speed of our departure to catch the Alamut bus from Qazvīn, we had not been able to find a bank to cash further traveller's cheques. Our existing supply of *rials* had only just met the First Muleteer's bill and left us enough to stand a few Pepsi Colas and take us on into Shahsāvar. Clearly his reward could not be in cash and must be in kind.

For us, one of the joys of travelling in the mountains had been a disregard of time. Our marches and halts were dictated by the daylight or the water springs, not by the clock. Yet the Second Muleteer had shown a touching interest in the precise time: he had made frequent enquiries, largely, we thought, as a simple conversational gambit. Caroline and I both wore men's wrist-watches – old but reliable ones of mine, which we viewed as robust rather than precious. It was the moment to part with one of them. We debated which, and decided to keep the one which I was wearing. Caroline unstrapped hers and handed it to me; I presented it with gestures of appreciation and friendship to the Second Muleteer.

His eyes lighted on it with longing, but he firmly refused to accept it. It was, he indicated, the lady's: he could not deprive her. Suspecting rightly that he would feel no such inhibitions in respect of me, I promptly undid my watch and strapped it on Caroline's wrist with an air of finality. Then I repeated my offer and it was accepted with unfeigned delight. Caroline and the Second Muleteer synchronized watches in an intimate little ceremony; we explained about winding, and had a race against the second hand to down a Pepsi Cola.

The bus for Shahsāvar, about whose existence we had been healthily sceptical, arrived in a cloud of dust which momentarily disguised the fact that it was a three-ton truck. The tailboard was lowered, our bags tossed up, the mules and donkey given a parting pat, the muleteers a final handshake, the time a final check, and then with a clatter and a roar we left for ever the shelter of the Elburz.

Chapter 5

Soltānīyeh and Tabrīz

Now, from the back of our truck, we saw for the first time the famous rice fields of the Caspian; it was this rice which had been conveyed on mule-back over the Elburz by the Salambar and other passes for centuries past. Tamerlane himself must have been tempted to traverse Persia by the Caspian shore and take advantage of such crops. But his preference for the inland route, south of the Elburz, may well have stemmed from a reluctance to face the torrid jungle of the Caspian coast, in which Tamerlane's cavalry would have been a prey both to brigands and to wild-life. Tigers infested the area in Tamerlane's time (and, indeed, until the late nineteenth century) but he preferred to hunt them in the grassy plains of the Qarabagh rather than among the dense foliage of the coast. The Tartars always preferred open country, either to campaign or to hunt over.

We were not left long for contemplation of the scenery. Our truck rounded a corner and we were confronted by an approaching vehicle. Instead of pulling in to the side of the road, our driver deliberately pulled into the centre and stopped. The approaching vehicle did the same. Everyone started shouting. Little by little we gathered the drift of the argument: our truck was the official bus, and our driver – loyally supported by his passengers – was protesting at the other lorry's carrying paying passengers. Maybe the legitimacy of his argument prevailed; or maybe there was relevance in the fact that our lorry was heavier than the oncoming one, and our driver larger than his opposite number. Whatever the reason, the opposing lorry pulled off the road; two passengers alighted and got into our lorry (which must surely have been very annoying for them, as presumably they wanted to go in precisely the opposite direction) and we trundled on. But not before our muleteers had overtaken us, with much merriment at the delays and hazards of the new-fangled means of travel we had adopted.

Shahsāvar is a watering place on the Caspian coast which doubtless has great charm for those who know it well. Certainly its streets, with their orange trees and Mediterranean appearance, raise expectations of the sybaritic life. We had been avidly looking forward to it ever since we left Gazar Khan, and dreaming of a hotel with clean sheets, hot water and plentiful food. Shahsāvar had become our Mecca. The reality was a bitter disappointment.

Having been put down by our lorry at what appeared to be the centre of the town, we explored by taxi and on foot the various hostelries to which we were directed. None seemed remotely appealing; perhaps it was too early in the season for the best of them to open. At all events we had a large meal (which managed to include no *mast*, unleavened bread or goat cheese) and then took a bus up the coast to Rasht, where we spent one night before going on by the road that runs back to Qazvīn. There was satisfaction in returning there, having achieved what we had set out to do. But we were not tempted to loiter: our next objective was Soltānīyeh.

Although he had prudently subjugated the valleys of the

Elburz and the forests of the Caspian coast, Tamerlane had taken as his main line of advance the old silk road running south of the mountains. It was at a staging post on this road that at the beginning of the fourteenth century the last of the Mongol invaders – Oljeitu – had built his magnificent mausoleum; at a green and shady haven, with good hunting in the surrounding hills and well-watered and cool in the summer. The place was called Soltānīyeh, and it was here that Tamerlane had in mind to leave the women of his harem: the last place on the road from Samarkand where they would be both safe and comfortable.

We know a good deal of what Soltānīyeh was like in Tamerlane's time, because the ambassador Clavijo passed through on his way to Tamerlane's court. He was sufficiently impressed with what he saw to describe it in considerable detail. He noted that it was a great caravan halt where the merchants from 'lesser India' (Afghanistan) brought spices, cloves, nutmeg and cinnamon; and where merchants from the shores of the Caspian and Caucasus brought silks. All these goods were bought by traders from Venice and Genoa. But the most romantic of the merchandise going through Soltānīyeh in Tamerlane's time were the precious stones. Rubies and pearls were sent by sea from China to Ormuz, the trading station at the mouth of the Persian Gulf visited by Marco Polo. From there it was a mere sixty days' camel ride to Soltānīyeh, where the gems were either traded with merchants from the West, or sold to any ladies of the Tartar court who might happen to be installed there waiting for their masters to return from campaigning.

It was not only the harem who were parked by Tamerlane at Soltānīyeh. His son – Prince Miram Shah – was holding court there when Clavijo was passing by on his journey to

Samarkand; and he sent emissaries to insist that Clavijo should break his journey to visit him. Since Clavijo was travelling with such exotic paraphernalia in the entourage of himself and his companions as a giraffe, several ostriches and some very fine falcons, it was little wonder that the Prince's curiosity overcame him.

Clavijo, who must have been a very effective intelligence agent as well as an admirable ambassador, as usual had an eye for the defences of the place. He noted that there were no town walls, but that there was a castle nearby. Presumably it was to this fortress that the ladies of Tamerlane's court repaired if there were rumours of trouble with the tribesmen from the Elburz mountains; but – as we have seen – Tamerlane did his best to ensure that such troubles should not occur.

The map today shows Soltānīyeh in fairly small type, and we had expected a modest-sized town on the road. It was therefore something of a surprise when our driver halted in the middle of what appeared to be a flat and featureless plain and announced 'Soltānīyeh', indicating that we should alight as he had stopped specially for us. Bewildered, we did as he requested; the bus pulled away leaving us, with our pseudo-Guccis, in a cloud of dust by the roadside.

As the dust settled, Caroline was the first to see it. A giant dome, two or three miles to the south of us, rose out of the flat countryside like a huge egg. Picking up our bags, we strode off down a sandy track in the direction of this intriguing landmark. Very soon a small truck, lurching and swaying uncertainly down the track behind us, stopped to offer us a lift. Gratefully we jumped aboard.

The one-time capital of the Mongol rulers of the Kingdom of Hulagu is today reduced to a tiny village of one-storey adobe huts, clustering at the foot of a monument. But what a monument it is! Nowhere in Persia, possibly nowhere else in Islam, is there so remarkable an architectural triumph as this 180-foot-high dome, supported on an octangular chamber 80 feet across inside, but much larger outside since the walls at their base are themselves 23 feet thick. The whole mausoleum is of brick and the dome is constructed as a single vault. It towers above the flat landscape, as improbable as it is remarkable.

It was clear as we approached the mausoleum through the crumbling village at its feet that extensive repair work was under way: scaffolding surrounded the dome. It was less clear how one could reach the building: a low wall with locked gates surrounded a forecourt. Everything looked deserted, so we climbed the low wall. Suddenly a figure appeared in one of the brick arches high above our heads and called out to us to wait. We sat patiently in the shade while he descended from his dizzy vantage point.

He was worth waiting for. Our guide, for so he became, was one of the team of craftsmen working on the restoration. He invited us to climb the long rickety ladders that led to high wooden platforms around the curve of the dome. As we climbed, he pointed out that if we examined the tilework we could read the names of Muhammad and his son-in-law Ali forming part of the pattern in several directions at once: the decorative mosaic was in fact a type of spiritual Scrabble board.

Descending to ground level again, he showed us how the removal of three-hundred-year-old plaster had revealed the original brickwork of the Mongol period. He pointed out piles of delicate peacock-blue tiles which were being used to re-surface the exterior of the dome, so that it would shine like a Fabergé egg from the distance at which – an hour before – we had first seen it. The tiles had been baked twice, for thirty hours each time, and would now withstand the rigours of the summer heat and winter cold on this exposed plain. Tiles from Isfahan, our guide told us, were incapable of surviving the winters here.

Caroline remarked that some of the patterns in the plaster work resembled carpets, and our guide confirmed that their Mongol creators had indeed taken their tribal rugs – the only patterns they knew – as their models.

Having completed our tour, Caroline was confronted with the problem of finding a position from which to photograph this mighty monument. The forecourt of the mausoleum was too close, and the tumbledown village beyond was too full of walls and roofs obscuring the view. The answer seemed to be to climb on to one of the roofs, and this we were attempting to do, amid the unhelpful merriment of an ever-increasing band of small children, when a diminutive boy with an authoritative air beckoned us round a corner to show us a ladder. Gratefully we climbed to a flat roof with an unparalleled view of Oljeitu's tomb. No sooner had we and our small companion ascended, than he pulled up the ladder behind us and we remained, undisturbed by the milling kindergarten below, for our photography.

But Ali, for such he told us was his name, had not completed his kindnesses yet. On the other side of the flat roof was the small interior courtyard of a modest adobe house. From a doorway in this emerged a smiling lady who, seeming quite unperturbed by the presence of strangers on her roof, signalled us to come down for a glass of tea. Spurning more conventional forms of entry, we lowered our ladder and accepted the invitation from – as it turned out – Ali's mother.

So dilapidated is the village of Soltānīyeh that it came as a surprise to find ourselves inside a clean and brightly carpeted room with a large family sitting cross-legged, or leaning against the familiar transparent plastic sheets which lined the walls to keep the insects in their place. We were ready for the hot, sweet tea and the proffered Turkish delight after our dusty walk. It was an occasion for a small present from us.

Persians take the whole question of giving and receiving presents extremely seriously. In fact, as Professor Browne pointed out in his *A Year Amongst the Persians* in 1893, there are no less than seven words for a present in Farsi. There is one word for the present you buy on a holiday or a pilgrimage to take home to your family, and another word for the present you might give them when you have not been away. There is a word for the present you give as a gesture of appreciation to someone who has done you a favour, and there is another word for the present that is given as a favour in the hope of a cash return. It is all very complicated and important if the wheels of social contact are to remain well oiled.

Although our performance with the wrist-watches might not suggest it, we had, in fact, a philosophy about presents, based on a rather personal interpretation of earlier travellers' practices. The traditional currency for travellers in the wilder parts of the Levant or the Orient was, of course, gold. As recently as the early years of this century, Gertrude Bell was carrying saddlebags of sovereigns around the Middle East, and in the 1930s Peter Fleming was carrying a small bar of gold (from which he shaved off fractions with a razor blade) across Tartary. We did not carry bullion.

But we did carry large quantities of a product invariably compared by its producer to gold. 'A little gold is always welcome . . . keep to the gold standard . . . nothing is as good as gold' – so ran a memorable series of advertisements for Benson & Hedges cigarettes in their distinctive gold boxes. And we treated the boxes as our bullion. A small favour would be recognized with the offer of a single cigarette; a larger favour would be rewarded with the gift of a pack of twenty; a major act of assistance would deserve a carton of two hundred. Everywhere they were acceptable and accepted, not so much for smoking – we suspected – as for passing on as currency within the system. They were light, easy to pack, easy to keep clean, relatively unbreakable and preserved their luxury appearance. We blessed Mr Benson and Mr Hedges frequently, as we left a glittering trail of their wares in our wake.

Inspired by the majesty of Oljeitu's Mongol monument, and heartened by the friendliness of our family in Soltānīyeh, we collected our bags from the tea house where we had left them and returned to the main road. It was not long before we prevailed on a smart Levantour bus to carry us north-west-wards on the next stage of our travels. We were now following directly the line of Tamerlane's main advance towards the first major objective of his campaign – the great city of Tabrīz, which had been captured and occupied by the Golden Horde.

Tabrīz in the late fourteenth century was possibly the largest city in the world, outside China. There were several more magnificent cities – Rome and Venice in the West, and Baghdad and Damascus in the East – but none to rival the bustle and prosperity of Tabrīz. This was where the east–west silk road crossed the north–south trade route from Russia to the Persian Gulf. Contemporaries estimated that Tabrīz had a population of one million souls and that the city comprised nearly a quarter of a million houses, not counting the tents of the itinerant population. Fra Oderic wrote in the fourteenth century that the revenues of the town of Tabrīz, presumably largely levies on the passing caravans, were more valuable than the annual revenue of the King of France. Ibn Batuta, a contemporary of Tamerlane's, described the exotic life and trade of the Tabrīz bazaar, with its musk markets and its trade in precious stones, its haughty Tartars and richly caparisoned slaves. He describes the mighty mosque of Ali Shah with its tall, clear marble columns, its tiled courtyards, its pools of ornamental water, and its gilded gateways. Clavijo was no less impressed: he observed 'a great palace with 20,000 rooms' at Tabrīz. All this opulence had been built up by the Mongol dynasty which immediately preceded Tamerlane.

It was therefore little wonder that Tamerlane resented the rape of Tabrīz by Tokhtamish, the leader of the Golden Horde who had been in former times a protégé of Tamerlane's. Not only was the seizure of such a city a material blow to the security and prosperity of the western marches of Tamerlane's empire, it was an affront to his *amour propre* and a sad loss to his exchequer.

Tokhtamish decided not to make a fight for Tabrīz. As Tamerlane approached, the Golden Horde evacuated the city and withdrew northwards into the shelter of the Caucasian mountains. The elders and people of Tabrīz quickly transferred their allegiance from one protector to another: they welcomed the new conqueror with open arms, feasts and celebrations.

Our own entry into the city was less spectacular, but – in its own way – equally friendly. Here for the first time since leaving Tehrān we encountered compatriots: John and Jill England of the British Council. We drank real scotch and slept in clean sheets. We were able to explain our curious quest in our own language to someone who not only understood but sympathized with our strange endeavours.

Not much remains today of the Mongols' and Tartars' Tabrīz, with one notable exception. The Ark (or Arg) remains a solid, indestructible monument to those stern masters of the city. It stands alone in a dusty, desolate open space in the centre of the city ('the most notable feature of which is a public lavatory', wrote Sir Roger Stevens) towering 120 feet into the air. This ancient citadel, which looked down on Tamerlane's entry in the summer of 1386, now frowned down on us as we stood blinking in the unsheltered sunlight. Until the beginning of this century, it had been customary to throw unfaithful wives from the summit of the Ark; one such lady managed to use her voluminous skirts as a parachute and by her spectacular and apparently miraculous escape, not only saved her life but redeemed her reputation. More recently still, during the uprising in Tabrīz in 1908 when the city was besieged by the Shah's troops, the Ark was used as a grain store and provisions were there protected against the hungry mobs rampaging in the streets.

If the city centre and monuments of Tabrīz were disappointing, at least there was one quarter of the city which had something of the feeling of the great trading junction which Tamerlane had come so far to reacquire. This was – predictably – the bazaar. Most Oriental bazaars are noisy, jostling places where the foreign visitor is plagued with the importunate attentions of vendors and small boys. Not so Tabrīz. Beneath its long, lofty brick archways there is no bustling but a constant rustle of quiet, purposeful movement, as the merchants and porters go about their serious business. No one cries his wares at the corner of the alleys, but there is a constant murmur of solemn bargaining. Far from accosting us, the traders of Tabrīz scarcely raised their eyes as we passed, despite the fact that we seemed to be the only foreigners to have penetrated their precinct on this bright May morning.

Off the main alleyways of the bazaar opened numerous large vaulted halls in which were piled carpets or other wares. In these cavernous interiors, lit with a dim religious light from skylights

The terrace of heads on the summit of Nemrut Dağ

The Armenian church on Akhtamar island in Lake Van

above, there was still an atmosphere of mystery and of wealth. Here in the bazaar one felt no surprise that Tamerlane had been able to extract a huge ransom from the citizens of the town he 'liberated' from the Golden Horde.

Tamerlane was expert at gauging the capacity of any town to pay for the lives and liberty of its burghers. In Tabrīz he was as thorough as later he was to be in Aleppo or Damascus. Having received the submission of the local emirs, he proceeded to receive the masters of each guild and craft separately. To each he dictated a price for survival, and from each he selected skilled craftsmen to be sent back to beautify his own capital:

> Then shall my native city Samarcanda . . .
> Be famous through the furthest continents.

These craftsmen were reluctant residents at Samarkand. Over one thousand master armourers were kept permanently incarcerated in the Ark there. Tamerlane also found it necessary to put armed guards on all boats on the Oxus to prevent fugitives from his capital attempting to return to their native regions of his empire. Samarkand may have been a golden city, but to many it appeared more like a gilded cage.

The first leg of Tamerlane's campaign was over. His court and army remained encamped around Tabrīz throughout the summer of 1386. The suppression of minor troubles in his rear, including the Elburz mountains despite the precautions he had taken, was directed from Tabrīz; the head of Emir Wali, a recalcitrant chieftain of that area, was brought to be laid at Tamerlane's feet there. All was under control.

And this was a rare state of affairs in the capital of Azerbaijan. The inhabitants of this corner of Persia have always been of an independent turn of mind and of an unusually diverse ethnic mix. Turkish-speaking Azerbaijanis, Kurds, Armenians, Persians, Georgians . . . all have rubbed shoulders in and around Tabrīz over the centuries between Tamerlane's visit and ours.

At one memorable moment in the early years of this century, Tabrīz set itself up as an independent nationalist centre of resistance to the despotic Qajar Shah. Happily for those interested in the more colourful moments of Tabrīz history, the British Consul-General of the moment – a certain A. C. Wratislaw, who never quite achieved a knighthood, despite a CB, CMG and CBE – wrote a lively account of those confused and doubtless alarming months of 1908.

The Shah's army besieged Tabrīz for considerably longer than Tamerlane required to do. The citizens were reduced to near starvation and threatened to attack the foreign consulates in order to provoke the intervention of Imperial Russian troops. The Kurdish tribesmen infesting the roads between Tabrīz and the Russian frontier plundered Royalists and Nationalists alike. Two Europeans, escaping to Russia, were stripped of all their clothing and sent on their way wearing only galoshes. Another family were faced with demands to surrender their child's nursemaid to a local chieftain's harem as the price of a safe-conduct; they declined but survived. One defeated commander of a Nationalist outpost was bastinadoed by his own side on returning to Tabrīz. Mullahs with Nationalist sympathies, when captured by the Royalists, were placed in tubs of water up to their necks and struck over the head with long poles whenever their heads appeared above water. The Shah maintained his unpaid troops with expectations of looting Tabrīz. Eventually, a combination of promises of constitutional reforms and – more immediately effective – the arrival of the Tsar's Cossacks, brought the siege to an end. Tamerlane had been fortunate that he had not had to fight against the deter-

mined citizens of this great junction on the world's highways
and history.

Our stay with John and Jill England at the British Council
house was calmer, and infused with a greater *rapport* with the
still unpredictable citizens of Tabrīz. To the Englands we con-
fided our tentative plans for the next stage of our journey.
Tamerlane had moved north-east from Tabrīz, pursuing the
Golden Horde into Georgia, that Christian kingdom of the
Caucasus whose mountains and rugged terrain surpassed even
that of the Elburz. We saw no prospect of being allowed to
explore the trail of Tamerlane where we would inside Russia.
On the other hand, we did particularly wish to reach the plains
of Qarabagh which lie across the frontier – half in Russia and
half in Iran – along the western edge of the Caspian Sea: these
plains had been important to Tamerlane, and therefore they
were important to us.

Chapter 6

To the Plains of Qarabagh

It was in the Qarabagh that Tamerlane preferred to winter on
this and other campaigns in the western marches of his empire.
The climate was milder than in the surrounding mountains,
and the road to home – through Soltānīyeh – was open. His
harem and the women of his army could be sent for. But, above
all, the Qarabagh was wonderful hunting country; and hunting
was his favourite pastime, apart from war. For the moment,
the pursuit of the Golden Horde was forgotten; it was as if
Tamerlane had decreed throughout his host:

> Hang up your weapons on Alcides' post;
> For Tamburlaine takes truce with all the world.

Tamerlane brought his own sense of style to his favourite
sport: it was all on a vast scale. A ring of hunters would be
thrown around several square miles of forest and tall grass. The
hunting animals would be assembled: mastiffs dressed in em-
broidered silks and leopards 'with chains of gold and collars set
with precious stones'. After three days and nights of working
inwards, beating the game into a concentrated circle, the hunters would close in for the kill. The bag would invariably include not only stags, gazelle and boar, but the tigers for which

the Qarabagh was famed. These last frightened even the intrepid Tartar horses, and obliged the hunters to mount Bactrian camels in rut, which were so ferocious that they were not unnerved even by tigers. The sheer volume of the bags would be immense; after all, they had to compare with the almost legendary bags recorded by some of the earlier Tartar conquerors, and it was still remembered that Genghis Khan's sons had sent him each week, as 'a sample of the game bag', fifty camel loads of swans.

Somehow we had to reach the Qarabagh. The first stage was to go to Ahar, a small town in the hills north-east of Tabrīz, and try to get assistance there to work our way further north. This would not be easy, because although we had no intention of entering the prohibited military frontier region, we knew that the closer we got to it, the more obstruction we might expect. John England introduced us to the Deputy Governor-General of the province, who promised to send a helpful message to the chief of gendarmerie at Ahar.

With this tenuous encouragement, we gratefully accepted a lift in John's Land Rover to an exceptionally chaotic bus station outside the city limits from which, rumour had it, local buses set off at unpredictable intervals to Ahar. The pseudo-Guccis found themselves strapped on the roof of a grey juggernaut which looked as if it had been assembled from the spare parts of other deceased buses (which it probably had been); and we found ourselves plonked, with many a friendly shove, through a surging mass of people and animals, into the seats immediately behind the driver. To the accompaniment of a noise that suggested that the driver would do well to look around for another gear-box soon, we were once more on our way.

We passed through low dusty hills, whose variegated colours indicated their rich mineral content, into more fertile country.

Camels grazed by the roadside. Bits fell off the bus. More passengers squeezed aboard. At the blind corners on the hill road, we wished that the courtesy of the country had not demanded that we should be quite so much in the front of the vehicle.

When we reached Ahar, we wasted no time in enquiring the way to the gendarmerie station. There we confidently expected official co-operation. We tidied ourselves up, so as not to let down the Deputy Governor-General; we looked, all things considered, reasonably spruce travellers as we presented ourselves to the sentry. We were therefore slightly disconcerted that he would not permit us to go up the garden path to the police station until we had left piled at his feet not only the pseudo-Guccis but Caroline's camera and handbag as well.

When our capacity to overthrow the forces of law and order in Ahar had thus been suitably reduced, we were escorted up the garden. Two quick glasses of tea later, we were being escorted down again, this time to a police jeep in which we set off to the local school to find an interpreter. The director of the Academy of Ahar was in the middle of an English class when the police posse arrived. They explained that his services were needed at the police station, and he explained that our services were needed at his English class. If he could exhibit us to his pupils first, he would gladly accompany us afterwards. This seemed only reasonable.

His wide-eyed pupils became even more wide-eyed at the sight of their first real Englishes. Would we, the director enquired, care to recite some Shakespeare? Nothing, I said, would give us greater pleasure; and I gave them an only slightly corrupt rendering of Macbeth's

> Is this a dagger which I see before me,
> The handle toward my hand. . . .

Half-way through it occurred to me that if our police escort understood any English at all, they might well decide they ought to frisk us even more carefully before we again entered their citadel.

In the jeep we explained to the schoolmaster the high historical seriousness of our journey. It would, we implied, be a great service to international scholarship if he could aid us on our way to the plains of Qarabagh.

The two hours which followed are not those which I shall remember as among the happiest of our journey. It seemed that the message from the Governor-General's office had not got through; that even if it had, the gendarmerie could not act on messages from any but their own headquarters; that there was no public transport going further up the road towards the Qarabagh; that in any case the road was very bad; that they would have been delighted to have sent us on our way in a police vehicle but they regretted they did not have the right documentation to explain our death on the road. (We protested that we did not intend to die on the road, but they said that did not alter the fact that if we did they needed the right papers to present with our corpses.) It was all very polite and very negative.

It was therefore in low spirits that we made our way to the hotel at Ahar. The price of a double room was, it appeared, only slightly less than that of a suite at the new Berkeley in London. The fact that there were no other visible guests and that the receptionist held a towel in front of the lower part of his face, both muffling his speech and engendering horrid forebodings about what ghastly – and infectious? – disfigurement was being concealed, did not altogether inspire enthusiasm for a long stay. We sat down in an empty hotel lobby and ordered a Coke; it cost exactly the price of a glass of champagne at White's.

We knew our luck had changed the moment he walked in. Eduardo was wearing a pair of faded blue jeans, a dusty sweat shirt and wrap-round dark glasses. He uttered an Iberian oath as he found himself unable to rouse Towel-mouth, and eased himself into a chair opposite us, smiling with the resignation of one who knows he is not exactly likely to find Hispanophone company at 6 p.m. on a Monday evening in Ahar. But he did. My rusty Spanish and Caroline's distinctive Portuguese were as welcome to him as his cheerful appearance was to us. Instantly we sensed an ally.

Eduardo told us his story. He was a geologist from Argentina, working for an American company on contract to the Iranian government to explore for uranium in the hills to the north of Ahar. He had a team of Chileans working for him; they had a camp near a tribal village an hour's drive away. He had come into Ahar to get some petrol and have a bath. He was going back to camp later the same night. Why didn't we leave our heavy luggage and join him?

Why not indeed? As we sat perched three abreast in the front of Eduardo's robust Chevrolet and drove into the Persian sunset, we experienced one of those moments of elation which make all the fatigue and frustration of Oriental travel a thousand times worth while.

'I don't know where we're going, or how far, or what we shall find when we get there,' said Caroline, 'but I know this is why we came.'

We were not disappointed. We stopped at Eduardo's camp just long enough to meet his companions who lived in a dormobile parked beside the track within view of a bore. Then Eduardo suggested that we should press on in the Chevrolet, fording an occasional stream, to a tribal village in the hills where, he told us, the headman was a friend of his, and where he had a standing invitation to dinner which would stretch to us too.

The American company who employed Eduardo knew how to pick their senior staff. I suspect he is a very good geologist; I am certain he would be a very good diplomat. Eduardo had early realized that much depended on his being able to leave extremely expensive machinery lying around on the Persian hillsides for weeks at a time. If things got stolen or broken, it would set his operation back by many weeks. So he had set about consolidating his relationships with the local villagers, winning their confidence and in turn their protection of his drills.

The sepia light was fading and the colour was draining out of the parchment landscape as the Chevrolet crested a hill, avoided an ugly-looking rock, and revealed below us a mud village that blended so precisely with its surroundings that no camouflage expert could have concealed it better. We had started to lurch down the track towards our goal, when we noticed a spurt of dust approaching us. Amid and generating the dust was a remarkably handsome stallion, and riding it an equally good-looking youth. He clattered to a standstill beside us, jumped off and greeted Eduardo like a brother. He escorted us into the village and straight to his own house.

The light was just enough to enable us to discern the colours and patterns of the intricate tribal rug which the youth's ten-year-old sister was weaving at a Heath-Robinson-like loom. This loom was a static one (as the villagers were not nomads) and thus both heavier and more delicate than many we were later to see being dismantled and placed on the back of a camel.

As we looked over the young girl's shoulder at her work, we

were reminded just how close to the Russian frontier we had come. Here on her loom were reproduced the classic Caucasian geometric motifs: eight-pointed stars, triangles and diamonds with a common vertex; borders of formalized 'serrated-leaf' and Kufic patterns (the last so named because of its resemblance to Kufic script). The nearby villages of Ardabil and Meshkin were renowned for developing their own variants on the more famous Shīrvān carpets which came from across the frontier. Much had changed in recent years even in these famous carpet centres, but here in the mountains the tribes still used the vegetable dyes which had been replaced elsewhere by chrome-based colourants. We were told that here blue was obtained from the leaves of the indigo plant; yellow came from vine leaves and saffron from weld; green was obtained by mixing yellow with the light blue derived from copper sulphate; black came from the natural wool of black sheep, and greys and browns were similarly derived from natural wool or else from the stain of walnut shells; and, lastly, reds were obtained from cochineal bugs or the blood of other insects. The availability of wool and these natural dyes contributed greatly to the carpet weavers' activity, but one ingredient was even more vital to the preservation of the ancient art – patience. As we watched the young girl's nimble fingers and far-away expression, we recognized that time was not a pressing factor in this distant corner of north-west Persia.

The little girl's father was headman of the village. He wore the clothes of a Persian peasant, but topped with an ancient grey trilby hat which he kept on indoors and out. He led us through the village to the stream whose banks formed the centre of community life: here the women of the village were filling water jars and collecting up washed clothes; here, too, horses and mules, sheep and goats were being watered. Thence we climbed to his own house: the mud-walled courtyard, the carpeted floor, the cellophane-covered interior walls, the plastic sheet laid in the centre of the room as a tablecloth, the cotton curtain across one corner where a few clothes were hung up . . . all these were reminiscent of Moghim's house at Gazar Khan.

But the meal was greatly superior to any we had consumed in such surroundings hitherto. The main dish was a pilaff with mutton and chicken, there were plentiful and delicious goat cheeses and great goblets of yogurt. With Eduardo's help we carried on a simple and appreciative conversation. It was now quite dark and our meal was interrupted by a growing circle of children who came in to view us, and of adults who came in to ask for the headman's decision on village matters. Once there was a document to be attested, and this he stamped with the print of his forefinger after an elaborate paste had been prepared from mud and chicken droppings.

It was time to bring in the animals. First the horses were led into the courtyard and tied up in a stable which ran along one side of it; then the mules; then the donkeys; and finally the whole of the remaining space in the courtyard was packed tight with the family's sheep.

We were just beginning to wonder how we would extricate ourselves through this mass of livestock, when our host – after much consultation with Eduardo – announced we were to be his guests for the night. We were so tired that we readily accepted the pile of carpets as a more welcome bed than anything the hotel at Ahar could have offered. Before Eduardo left us, he arranged that on the morrow the villagers would help us find a way across the hills towards the Qarabagh.

The next day was a golden one from the start. And the start was 5.30 a.m. when the sheep were let out of the yard. In the half-light, the whole village seemed a sea of moving animals: they streamed out through the mud walls and were swallowed up in the grey grasslands. This was life as it had been by the Sea of Galilee two thousand years ago. A dog barked, a horse neighed, a child cried: the inexorable process of another day in eternity had begun.

We wandered unheeded through the village and returned to our house to find that the women had already gathered up all the animal droppings of the previous night from the courtyard and carefully stacked them to meet future fuel needs; they had also prepared glasses of hot tea. While we were drinking these, our host's son clattered into the courtyard, on the same fine stallion on which we had encountered him the previous day; he was leading two frisky geldings. He pointed to the horizon with a histrionic gesture which created the sensation of our having somehow encountered Omar Sharif in the midst of a dramatic sequence in the filming of *Lawrence of Arabia*, and then declaimed 'To Qarabagh!'

We would return to the village, he said, so no farewells were needed. After stuffing sheets of unleavened bread into a saddle-bag, and checking that our water-bottles were full, he gallantly gave Caroline a leg up on to one of the horses and held the head of mine while I mounted. It was 6.30 a.m.

It is not really very comfortable to ride for eleven hours when you have spent most of the previous days cooped up in Persian buses or recovering from walking over mountains. It was a day of mind over matter. The excitement of wondering what lay beyond every crest of the hills helped us to forget the stresses and strains of what lay below our waists.

Omar (for so we christened him between ourselves as we could not get his real name around our tongues) was a good guide – more intelligent than our muleteers had been, and less demanding in his interrogation of us than Moghim. His keen eyes spotted things we would have missed: an eagle hovering over some young lambs, a plume of smoke from a village on the horizon. Shortly after midday, when the sun was shimmering down on the silvery grey hills, Omar pointed out the head of a camel train rounding the shoulder of a distant hill. The line of camels, broken by mules and men on foot, seemed to uncoil from the hill indefinitely till it stretched for more than half a mile.

Caroline, a childhood of hunting in Ireland standing her in good stead, suggested that we should gallop over to meet the camel train. The idea, if not the rapid motion it would involve, appealed to me too. But Omar would not permit it. The camel train was a fragment of the Shahsavan tribe, a nomadic people whose name denotes their historic loyalty to successive Shahs, but who – it appeared – were no friends of Omar's village. It seemed they grazed their animals on the home lands of settled farmers, and might interpret a sudden visit by three horsemen as an unwelcome protest. As the sun glistened on their colourful costumes, we regretted these local frictions; but prudence and deference to Omar's views prevailed. The Shahsavan snaked their way into invisibility.

After our lunch of flat discs of unleavened bread, we began climbing more seriously. Even Omar's stallion was beginning to lather up. At the crest of the next hill we tethered the horses to pegs which we drove into the hard ground, but which would scarcely have impeded them had they decided on flight. Then we scrambled up an outcrop of rock and followed with our eyes the line of Omar's pointing arm. The far distance was no longer grey, silver or brown: it was unmistakably green. We had seen the plains of Qarabagh.

Chapter 7

Caucasian Interlude

To go down to the plains was out of the question. We would be entering a border area and be liable to arrest by the military. Worse, if we evaded the Iranian military we might stray into the Soviet Union like Aunt Dot and the Reverend Father Chantrey-Pig in Rose Macaulay's *Towers of Trebizond*. Also, if we went further we would not get back to Omar's village before nightfall. Wistfully we rejoined the horses and turned towards the south-west again.

I mused much on the long ride back about the terrain beyond: we had seen the southern fringe of the Plains of Qarabagh and – in their northern part – these plains stretched into the Russian Caucasus. It was into these Caucasian mountain fastnesses that the Golden Horde had retreated after Tamerlane's arrival before the gates of Tabrīz. Tamerlane had pursued them. And there had been further reasons for him to press on into the Caucasus: the kingdom of Georgia was a Christian kingdom and, as a self-appointed champion of Islam, Tamerlane always argued that fighting Christians – like defending pilgrim routes – lent a special justification to a campaign. So Tamerlane, having spent much of the summer of 1386 around Tabrīz or hunting in the Qarabagh, when the autumn came appointed Muhammad-Sultan as governor of Tabrīz and himself led his army northwards through the Caucasian mountains.

His first objective was Tiflis (now Tbilisi), the chief fortress of King Bagrat's kingdom of Georgia. Tamerlane laid siege to the town – the first full-scale siege of the campaign. He had already developed a certain ritual about sieges. He gave his opponents warning of his intentions by the colour of his accoutrements: when he was encamped in white tents, he was open to receive the surrender offers of his antagonists, in which case there would be heavy ransoms to pay but no general pillage or slaughter. He would send heralds with solemn warnings, and would march around the threatened town or castle displaying both the extent of his force and the nature of his siege equipment. The seven-foot-long Tartar trumpets would sound their menacing note. What happened next was an ominous change of battle colours, best described by a messenger in Marlowe's *Tamburlaine the Great*:

> But if these threats move not submission,
> Black are his colours, black pavilion;
> His spear, his shield, his horse, his armour, plumes,
> And jetty feathers menace death and hell;
> Without respect of sex, degree or age,
> He razeth all his foes with fire and sword.

This procedure was followed at Tiflis, but Bagrat declined to surrender.

Tamerlane now moved into his next phase. He called up the assault machines and loaded his catapults with rocks from the surrounding hills. The battering-rams hammered at the gates; the stones from the catapults thundered on to the heads of the defendants; flaming bundles of hay were showered on the wooden galleries along the walls; the engineers burrowed under the walls. When everything had been done both literally and metaphorically to undermine the defences, Tamerlane himself led the assault on the citadel. Protecting his head with a wattle shield from the showers of arrows that descended from the ramparts, Tamerlane forced an entry. His hold over his troops was in large measure based throughout his career on those qualities of personal fearlessness which had distinguished him as the leader of a marauding band in his youth. Frequently wounded, often suffering the loss of his charger, habitually in the hottest part of the battle, and unmoved by suffering in others or in himself, he would truly have been entitled to say:

> For he shall wear the crown of Persia
> Whose head hath deepest scars, whose breast most wounds,
> Which, being wroth, sends lightning from his eyes,
> And in the furrows of his frowning brows
> Harbours revenge, war, death and cruelty;
> For in a field, whose superficies
> Is covered with a liquid purple veil,
> And sprinkled with the brains of slaughtered men,
> My royal chair of state shall be advanc'd;
> And he that means to place himself therein,
> Must armed wade up to the chin in blood.

Tiflis, despite its strong position on the banks of the Kura river, was taken by storm. King Bagrat and his family were captured and put in fetters; the town was sacked and many of the dark-eyed Georgian maidens carried off and sent back to the Tartar camp in the Qarabagh, to which Tamerlane himself now withdrew to spend the winter.

It was to the Qarabagh that King Bagrat was brought to

Tamerlane's presence. The latter had determined on the conversion to Islam of the king of Georgia and – according to Sharaf al-din – gave him 'a thousand good reasons for renouncing his Christian faith'. It was a difficult decision for Bagrat. On the one hand, he came from a uniquely long line of Christian descent: his family claimed the Virgin Mother as a relation of their ancestors, and, indeed, members of the Georgian royal House of Bagration used to wear black at the feast of the Assumption of the Virgin (as recently as until the Russian Revolution) on the grounds that they 'were mourning for a family bereavement' on that date. On the other hand, Tamerlane promised Bagrat that if he renounced his faith he would be restored to his kingdom – albeit as a vassal of Tamerlane – and that he would receive gifts and honours from his conqueror. We do not know what threats formed the obverse of these inducements: Tamerlane could be very persuasive.

Bagrat abjured his Christianity and, in his anxiety to persuade Tamerlane of the strength and permanence of his decision, presented the conqueror with the most holy relic he possessed – a coat of chain-mail which was believed to have been forged by the prophet David with his own hands and for his own use in battle against the Philistines. Grand gifts and memorable gestures were a sure way to Tamerlane's favour.

The king of Shīrvān had observed this and realized that he was likely to follow the same fate as the king of Georgia. Just as the fortress town of Tiflis was essential to Tamerlane's control of the routes through the Caucasus, so was the Darband Pass that ran through the kingdom of Shīrvān essential to Tamerlane's plan to protect his empire from further incursions from the north. Rather than wait to be attacked and cast into fetters like his fellow monarch, the king of Shīrvān surrendered his territory and arrived at Tamerlane's court with rich gifts. It

G

was customary for royal presents to be made in batches of nine: nine richly caparisoned horses, nine golden goblets, nine daggers mounted with precious stones. All these the king of Shīrvān presented, but when he came to hand over a gift of slaves, there were only eight of them. Tamerlane remarked on the unaccustomed deficiency, and the king of Shīrvān promptly replied that he offered himself as the ninth of Tamerlane's slaves. The remark was as great a success as King David's suit of chain-mail had been.

But despite the submission of other rulers too, including the princes of the coastal provinces of Gilan, Tokhtamish continued to harass the northern Caucasus and Tamerlane felt obliged to interrupt his festivities in the Qarabagh to send further expeditions in this direction. The country they covered was old in history before then, and rich in romance in more recent centuries.

I had already covered this Caucasian territory of Tamerlane's campaign on a previous expedition of my own. Had it not been so, I would have felt our present itinerary incomplete; as it was, I found myself recalling vividly the detail of that earlier journey, as I rode back towards Omar's village. I had been a young diplomat in Russia for the first time; much had changed elsewhere in the intervening years, but I knew that very little would have changed in the mountain fastnesses of the Caucasus, and it would be now as I remembered it then.

I had gone north from Tiflis as Tamerlane had done, travelling along the same route but by the Georgian Military Highway. This remarkable road was begun in 1783 by Count Paul Potemkin, a cousin of Catherine the Great's celebrated lover. He mobilized eight hundred Russian soldiers to convert the rough bridle paths, along which Tamerlane and all previous conquerors of the Caucasus had led their armies over the

mountains, into a road across which he could march his bat-
talions and trundle not only heavy field-guns but his own
carriage, drawn by eight horses, from Vladikavkaz to Tiflis.
The highway was to be completed in the 1820s by that greatest
of all Russian commanders in the Caucasus, General Yermolov.

The first place I had passed on leaving Tiflis towards the
north was a town given its death blow by Tamerlane. Mtskheta
was the ancient capital of Georgia when the Tartars attacked
and destroyed it. Nothing remained of the fourteenth-century
town when I was there, though there was much masonry from
later periods, and I recall that it still had a fortified look, as if it
awaited further assaults from intruders: the old cathedral
church of Sveti Tzkhoveli still sported crenellated outer walls
and watch towers. It was after Tamerlane's attentions that the
capital of Georgia was permanently moved to Tiflis, which
though ravaged had been less utterly devastated.

The next notable landmark along the Highway, in my day
as in Tamerlane's, was the castle of Ananuri, whose tall and
formidable keep had failed to halt the advancing Tartars. Even
in a region renowned, like the Scottish Borders, for its romantic
towers, Ananuri is celebrated – perhaps most for an episode in
1727. The occupant of the castle, a certain Prince Bardsig, was
carousing with his cronies when they spied the beautiful young
wife of a neighbouring prince riding up the valley with her
chaplain and falconers. It was the work of a moment for Prince
Bardsig and his companions to mount their horses, ambush the
visiting party, chase off the chaplain and falconers, and carry
the young princess back to their castle. This was a conventional
affront; the story only became remarkable when the princess's
seduction was flaunted by the flying of her pink pantaloons
from the flagpole on the castle keep. Although she was subsequently returned to her husband, the pantaloons continued to

fly over Ananuri; until her husband swore he would replace them with the head of Prince Bardsig. A siege, a storm and a massacre followed, before eventually a gory severed head replaced the provocative pink pantaloons. Such was ever life in the Caucasian mountains.

Having crossed the watershed of the Caucasian range, the Military Highway begins to follow the valley of the Terek – a river for ever associated with Tamerlane as the scene of his greatest victory over the Golden Horde. Here the mountains become bleaker, the slopes steeper and the road narrower. My own crossing had been in late autumn and I well remember spending many hours firmly stuck in flocks of sheep being driven down from the mountains to their winter pastures in the valleys below, the rumble of the Terek rising from the gorges below us.

In his campaign of 1386, Tamerlane had never caught up with the Golden Horde; they had withdrawn further north than he wished to pursue them. It was in a later campaign – that of 1395 – that Tamerlane effected his famous trickery on the banks of the Terek. The armies of Tamerlane and of the Golden Horde had been following opposite banks of the river and were encamped facing each other at a point where the torrent was too wide and fierce to allow of any crossing. After night had fallen, Tamerlane led his warriors out of the camp and back along their tracks to a ford where he crossed over to the enemy's side of the river. Meanwhile he had left all the non-combatants behind in his camp, instructing them to keep their fires well stoked and the noisy clatter of camp life going throughout the night. The element of surprise he achieved by falling on the Golden Horde while they still imagined he was encamped opposite, and out of reach of them, was the decisive factor in his victory.

But now the river Terek was entering the Lermontov country. Where it passed through the Darial Gorge, with its jagged peaks above the precarious road, the ruins of the fabled castle of Queen Tamara could be seen. The poet Lermontov wrote in *The Demon* of how Tamara had had her rejected lovers cast from this spectacular point to their deaths in the gorge below. I recall the place and the story well, since my own knowledge of the Russian language was based on a stay with an exiled Georgian princess – also called Tamara – in Paris only a few months before my crossing of the Georgian Military Highway. Tamerlane would have passed the castle, and no doubt played his own familiar part in reducing it to its present ruins.

The exact point at which Tamerlane turned south again on his 1386 campaign has never been determined. I like to think it was at Pyartigorsk, a romantic little town named after the five hills among which it stands, because this is where I had ended my own transcaucasian crossing. Pyartigorsk would have been a logical place for Tamerlane to turn, as it constitutes part of the frontier between Georgia and what has always been Russia: the Cossack line once ran near to here. It is best remembered for being the scene of Lermontov's death in a duel, and a statue commemorates the spot where he fell. It should also be remembered for being the scene of many of the earlier escapades of this dashing cavalry officer, revolutionary and poet whose life alternated between the glittering palaces of St Petersburg and – whenever he fell from favour with the Tsar – the rugged life of military campaigning in the Caucasus. At the tiny spa of Pyartigorsk, Lermontov recovered from his campaigns, gambled, made love, wrote romantic poetry and picked fatal quarrels with his fellow officers.

My own experience of Pyartigorsk on my earlier expedition had been comic rather than tragic. I was accompanying the

British Ambassador and we both arrived weary after a long day's travel. We were received courteously by the dignitaries of this small watering place and led to a Soviet government guest house where we were to spend the night. Here the mayor and corporation of Pyartigorsk, still attentively accompanying us, said they would like to ask us a favour: they explained that the guest house had a billiard room and a full-sized billiard table; this was a relic of the last days of the Tsarist regime when the house had been the residence of a high state official; the billiard table, cues and balls had been scrupulously preserved . . . but no one in Pyartigorsk knew how to play the game. It was, they understood, a very English game, and much played in London clubs: could we give them a demonstration? Indeed, they added, our visit had been eagerly awaited as an incomparable opportunity to see an exhibition match.

The Ambassador and I looked at each other in consternation: neither of us played billiards nor even knew the rules. But we could not disappoint our Soviet hosts or shatter their illusions of London club life. We thought of England and reached for the cues: balls cannoned off cushions, some struck each other and some even went into pockets. Happily no green baize was torn. We made up the rules as we went along. Puzzled expressions spread over the broad faces of the mayor and corporation of Pyartigorsk; billiards was declared to be a very complicated game. But honour was satisfied: we were allowed to retire to bed.

But whether it was at Pyartigorsk or at some other strategic turning place, Tamerlane decided in the early months of 1387 that he was not yet ready to make a full-scale campaign in pursuit of Tokhtamish and the Golden Horde inside Russia. He had reoccupied Tabrīz; he had chased the Golden Horde out of the Caucasus; he had brought to submission the independent kingdoms of the region; he had provided some excellent sport for his emirs and his soldiers on the hunting fields of the Qarabagh; he had sent back skilled craftsmen and rich spoils to Samarkand. Besides, there were temptations further west. The word of command went out:

> Now will we banquet on these plains a while,
> And after march to Turkey with our camp. . . .

Chapter 8

Into Asia Minor

Tamerlane could not claim that his campaign across Armenia westwards into Asia Minor was a holy war for Islam, since – unlike the Christians of Georgia – the Turkoman tribes were followers of the Prophet. But they were behaving in a manner which suggested to Tamerlane that they were forgetful of this fact: they were menacing the pilgrim routes to Mecca. More important no doubt to Tamerlane's private calculations, they were also menacing the profitable caravan routes across Asia Minor which supplied the western marches of his empire. It was the fatal and familiar combination of activities which provided for Tamerlane both a pretext and a motive for intervention.

The temptation to intervene was the greater because the Turkoman tribes were divided among themselves into two rival, and frequently warring, confederations: the Black Sheep and the White Sheep. The leader of the former group of tribes – Qara-Muhammad – had committed two dangerous errors: he had supported Sultan Ahmad Jalayir when the latter had taken power in Tabrīz in opposition to the Tartar overlords, and he had failed to answer a summons to appear before Tamerlane and make his submission. A punitive expedition was indicated.

Caroline and I had returned from Omar's village to Ahar, and from there to Tabrīz. Now we planned to follow Tamerlane's march westwards taking advantage – for once – of the fact that his route coincided with a good modern road as far as Erzurum. The obvious form of transport for us was a long-distance bus, preferably one which crossed the frontier from Iran to Turkey with its passengers, because we had heard of the fate of travellers deposited at the frontier point (several miles from any village) who then fell victim to extortionate demands from local carriers – with carts, lorries or taxis – on whom they were dependent for getting to some point of human habitation.

But such buses were about as rare as good post horses in Tamerlane's day. There was one which, we were told, left Tabrīz at 5.30 a.m. (which seemed to be becoming our normal start time); we should be at the bus depot at five to get a seat. Nothing daunted, we set our alarm clock for four; packed, made ourselves strong coffee and tiptoed out of the Englands' compound into the dark, chilly, pre-dawn city. It seemed we had been well informed: the depot was a hive of activity at 5 a.m. We bought some Turkish delight (no substitute for cornflakes and marmalade, but all that was available) and supervised the loading of our bags on to the roof of the bus. At 5.45 a.m. we set off. At 5.52 a.m. we stopped again; everyone debussed for tea and yogurt. We made two more stops in Tabrīz: once to collect passengers who were friends of the driver, and once to say goodbye to some mate of the driver who did not appear to have gone to bed yet. The sun was up by the time we nosed our way out of Tabrīz towards Khvoy.

We were now also travelling – albeit in the opposite direction – along the route which Ambassador Clavijo had taken on his mission to Tamerlane in 1404. Clavijo, as we have already seen, had made notes about every settlement of any significance which he passed, and more particularly about their defences.

At Khvoy we saw what we thought might have been the remains of Clavijo's 'wall of baked bricks, with many towers and barbicans'. But we looked in vain for the minaret of human skulls which Tamerlane had left there as a warning to passers-by of the fate which awaited those who stirred up trouble in his rear. We hunted so assiduously that not only did we almost miss our bus, but I fear we finally convinced the sober citizens of Khvoy that the English were as mad as they had always suspected: sign language, we reluctantly concluded, is an inadequate medium for seeking directions to a minaret of skulls.

But if the inhabitants of Khvoy thought we were bizarre, their surprise can have been as nothing compared to that which they evinced on the occasion of Clavijo's visit. And it was not the Spanish envoy who must have astounded them, but his *cher collègue* an Egyptian ambassador, also bound for Tamerlane's court, whose caravan met Clavijo's at this improbable rendezvous. The Egyptian's gifts from his sultan were far more opulent and unusual than Clavijo's own falcons, silver and broadcloth: the Egyptian's *pièce de résistance* was nothing less than a giraffe, which was made to walk as part of the caravan from Cairo to Samarkand. He had also brought ostriches for good measure, though presumably these were transported rather than expected to walk. Clavijo himself was almost as intrigued at first view by the giraffe as were the local citizenry of Khvoy. He describes it meticulously: 'When the beast raised its head, it was a wonder to see the length of the neck, which was very thin and the head somewhat like that of a deer. The hind legs in comparison with the forelegs were short, so that anyone seeing the animal casually for the first time would imagine it to be seated and not standing ... its neck can overtop any wall ... a very wondrous sight to behold.'

After Khvoy, the scenery became wilder. On either side of the road were caves and sudden hidden valleys: this was robber baron country. We passed through Mākū, a village set in a gorge with rock faces rising steeply behind its few houses. And then through the clouds we saw our first glimpse of Mount Ararat looming above us to the north, like a mighty sentinel watching over the meeting place of Russia, Persia and Turkey. I regretted that from this angle we would be unable to see the cleft in the mountain which has perhaps the most romantic association of any natural phenomenon: it is supposed to be the groove left by the keel of Noah's Ark, as that heavily laden vessel found its final resting place after the flood.

We did, however, see a ruin on the lower slopes of Mount Ararat which we were told by one of our fellow passengers (not altogether convincingly) was that of the Castle of Iğdir. This castle had been captured by Tamerlane, and after he had slain its lord he had left the widow in charge of the castle – on the condition that all the doors and gates should be permanently removed. Clavijo had spent a draughty night there on his way from Erzurum to Khvoy.

Now our proximity to the frontier was borne in on us by less attractive and more modern evidence of transport problems. We started passing the tail of a queue of lorries several miles before we reached the border, and we counted 411 on the Iranian side (we were later to find another 170 on the Turkish side waiting to enter Iran), many of them from Bulgaria and Romania and some from even more improbable places of origin. We were told by our fellow passengers that in high summer the queue became even longer and that some drivers were obliged to wait as long as three weeks to complete the crossing and its attendant formalities.

When our own bus reached the crossing point (only lorries queued) we drove into a large concrete yard with a gate in the middle. The far side of the gate was Turkey, and through this our bus would pass as soon as it had been examined. We were to debus in the yard, enter a side building, pass through passport control and customs and emerge in the yard on the far side of the gate to rejoin our bus in Turkey. Nothing could have seemed neater, but this little manoeuvre took us two and a quarter hours of hard application.

To start with, reaching the shelter of the passport control building, having emerged from the bus, was no simple task. While we and our fellow passengers gesticulated at our luggage on the roof, huge articulated lorries bore down on us in the crowded, sweltering yard. Others backed with blind abandon into standing groups of passengers, who scattered, littering their bags in their wake. The yard had the appearance of an army's baggage train which had just been overrun by a squadron of Cossacks.

As we gained the shelter of the building, Caroline enquired whether there was a loo. It seemed an unnecessary question as the atmosphere indicated there not only was one but that it was located near at hand. Her subsequent description of it defied repetition.

'Since they give us slippers in the hotel bedrooms, I wonder why they don't issue gum boots in the loos,' she said wistfully.

In the Iranian emigration we had a much easier time of it than some Kurds on our bus, whose documentation seemed to be non-existent or, at best, highly questionable. But when we reached the Turkish immigration, a scene ensued which was to become increasingly familiar. It was largely the fault of my own passport.

Over years of travelling in the Diplomatic Service, I have acquired visas, some of which the Foreign Office in their wisdom tell me should be kept in my current passport; so when it gets filled up, instead of replacing it with a new one, they attach a new one to the front. This has happened twice and the resultant book – three passports thick – will not fit in any pocket. Worse, it presents the frontier official of enquiring mind with 96 pages of apparently enthralling literature.

The Turkish official settled down for a good read. In a desultory sort of way he appeared to be looking for an appropriate place to implant his rubber entry stamp, but he was easily deflected. What was this, he asked, pointing to a cancelled Polish diplomatic visa? Why was my Ruanda visa (No. 10,004 – issued two days after Independence and really, I suspected, No. 4) written in long-hand? It was useless to explain that these esoteric souvenirs of bygone frontier dramas were, perhaps, irrelevant to the purpose in hand. Had I not given him the passport to read? He must satisfy himself about it. Eventually he crashed his imposing stamp on to the page – in fact a page hitherto reserved for the inscription of traveller's cheques issued under the Exchange Control Regulations.

But we were not done. Details from the voluminous passport had to be inscribed on to a lengthy form. Here again life was not straightforward. When the most recent of my passports was issued, the initials MVO (representing the modest distinction of Member of the Royal Victorian Order) were written in bold green letters after my name in the window provided on the cover. I could see that it was this appellation which was being carefully copied on to the form under the heading 'family name'. And why not indeed? 'MVO' must have seemed no more improbable than 'URE' – indeed in many parts of the world (including Africa, but not including Argyll whence my my name originates) the former seems both more pronounceable and to carry greater probability. I let it go, wondering vaguely whether we would be obliged for the duration of our time in Turkey to sign ourselves into hotels as Mr and Mrs Mvo.

Caroline's passport, a more slender and virginal document, aroused less curiosity. Indeed the only problem we have ever had with hers was when a minor official at an unauthorized road block attempted to prize her photograph off the page because, he explained disarmingly, he wanted to keep it among the souvenirs in his wallet. No such attempt was made on this occasion.

Eventually we emerged blinking into the harsh sunlight on the Turkish side of the yard. Another hour of buying sweet biscuits and even sweeter orange drink, and we were once more on our way, passing a steady flow of lorries in the opposite direction, which was presumably the modern equivalent of the 'endless caravans of camels transporting European goods to northern Persia' encountered by Mr Consul Wratislaw when he had travelled these roads.

After passing through the small Turkish town of Ağri, our driver elected to leave the main road and take to an earth road to its south, which, he said, was a more direct route to Erzurum. This may have been strictly true, and indeed our new unmade road was attended by so much rock blasting (some of it on high defiles above the road and much too close for comfort) that it seems likely that it is to be the line of the new trunk road from Turkey to Iran. But whatever the future prospects of the road, the present condition of it deteriorated the further we progressed. Eventually, in an effort to pass a tractor, we got finally stuck and everyone had to debus and push in the mud, while a

sudden rainstorm added to our difficulties. Several times horsemen passed on the ridges above the road and eyed us at our
labours; any thoughts of plunder they might have had were
clearly deterred by the sight of our sodden baggage and mud-
splashed clothing.

Clavijo had been less lucky in the mountains approaching
Erzurum. It was here that he and his entourage had been stopped
by a local robber chief who had explained that the visitors were
passing through his territory and that it was very difficult to
make a living in the area unless visitors were generous enough
to give donations to him to ensure their protection. Clavijo
succumbed to this veiled threat by surrendering a silver goblet
– doubtless one of the many objects he had brought with him
to give away in just such an eventuality. However, the local
chief felt that this was an inadequate contribution and declined
to let Clavijo pass until he had also handed over several lengths
of scarlet cloth. As the local horsemen gazed down disdainfully
at us floundering in the mud, I felt convinced they were con-
cluding that we had little scarlet cloth and fewer silver goblets
in our tattered and squelching pseudo-Gucci luggage.

We had been travelling for thirteen hours when our bus
finally trundled into Erzurum. We saw nothing of Clavijo's
'very broad strong stone wall with many towers' (which did
not seem to do the town much good: it held out less than a day
against Tamerlane) but found the streets alive with Turkish
soldiers, as befitted a garrison town which had seen its share of
invaders over the centuries. We decided to postpone our ex-
amination of the place until we had had some sleep.

We woke in Erzurum on a clear sunny morning and from
our bedroom window we could see the snow-capped hills
immediately beyond the town. At 6,200 feet above sea level,
with its surrounding hills rising to 8,000 feet, Erzurum has

the sparkling air of a skiing resort. The winters there can be long and hard, but now it was spring and all our weariness of the previous night was dispelled in the tingling mountain atmosphere.

The major sight of Erzurum is the same now as it was when the vanguard of Tamerlane's cavalry thundered into the town in the spring of 1387: the Cifte Minareli Medrese. It was towards this mosque, mausoleum and museum in one that we directed our post-breakfast steps. The Cifte Minareli Medrese was founded in 1253 by the Seljuk Sultan Alaeddin Keykubad II in honour of his daughter, whose mausoleum is part of the structure. The building is easy to recognize on account of its distinctive twin minarets at either side of a splendidly proportioned Seljuk entrance-way. Inside, the long rectangular court has two-storeyed porticoes, with an *iwan* at either side. Rough-hewn wooden scaffolding, so heavy that it was difficult to tell if this was to support the weight of the repair workers or of the building itself, loomed above us. The whole effect was powerful, massive and louring, as if it were designed to demonstrate to us as to Tamerlane that the Seljuk civilization, although it might be overthrown, could never be annihilated.

The portal of the Cifte Minareli Medrese is still the town meeting place of Erzurum. Old, bearded and beturbaned men, sitting on benches outside and blinking like owls in the morning sunshine, discussed the frivolities and transience of modern life – much as their predecessors had doubtless done for seven centuries. The women had less leisure to sit and stare: they walked about with a purposeful air, their faces hidden within all-enveloping *charshafs* which appeared to be made not of the customary black cloth but of distinctive russet-coloured sacking material. Caroline was more cautious about photographing them than the men: the mild-looking matrons of Erzurum

The ruined castle on the Rock of Van, captured by Tamerlane

A fellow traveller across Kurdistan

have a reputation for savage treatment of hostile intruders. Wratislaw recorded that: 'After the desperate efforts of the Russians in 1878 to take the Deve Boyoun pass, these same bundles sallied out of the town in hundreds to mutilate and murder the unfortunate Russian wounded.'

Erzurum has been a garrison town for most of its long history: Seljuks and Ottomans, Cossacks and Tartars, Arabs and Armenians have flowed over and through this mountain citadel. Our guide-book told us that 'it is becoming less noticeably a garrison town': certainly the old fort no longer had a sentry at the gate; its only armament was an abandoned nineteenth-century field-gun on the barrack square, and there was washing hanging out from the old guard house. But the cafés were still full of tough, serious-looking soldiers, and we formed the firm impression that any latter-day Tamerlane would be left in no doubt as to who now controls Erzurum.

Tamerlane's army had spread out from Erzurum, some squadrons of cavalry riding north-west towards Trebizond, but the main body – under the command of their leader – circling south towards Lake Van and the most intransigent fortress in all Armenia.

Trebizond was a temptation. We knew that another day's bus ride through the Çoruh mountains would bring us to this ancient capital of the Comnene empire, with its towers immortalized by Rose Macaulay, with its Byzantine churches, once bustling port and lively markets. We knew that we would be treading the route taken by the survivors of Xenophon's campaign against the Persians; by Clavijo; by Joseph Wolff; and by the less-renowned but ever-intrepid Mr Consul Wratislaw who had made the journey in 1887, taking a week in a 'four-wheeler closed cab' and stopping for the nights at *hans* which he describes as 'little more than sheds divided up into

compartments, indescribably dirty and swarming with preda-
tory insects'.

Caroline and I had spent a busy morning of photography
and sightseeing in Erzurum and we felt we had earned a good
lunch over which to discuss our next move. Caroline was for
heading for Trebizond (or Trabzon as we now found it marked
on our maps); while I was for sticking to the authentic route
(so far as it could be determined) of Tamerlane himself, and
going as directly as possible to Lake Van in the south-east.
We spread out our maps. The more we studied the possibilities,
the harder my idea appeared: there were no direct routes to
Lake Van, but a succession of winding roads none of them
taking less than 250 miles to cover the 100 miles as the crow –
or more likely the eagle in this part of the world – flies.

We decided to go down to the bus depot and ask about
possibilities. Normally, I find Turkish bus depots are perhaps
the places closest of all to the pulse of that country: there is a
purposeful confusion, a classless mêlée, a making of noise for
its own sake which is at once excruciating and endearing.
They have the tension of a nineteenth-century railway station:
every long-distance bus is a miniature Orient Express. My
favourite bus depot in all the world is Izmir (or Smyrna to give
it its more traditional and evocative name) and the best time to
be there is midnight. Buses are leaving for every destination in
the Near East and every bus company has its own booth, resembling a bookie's stand at a racecourse, from which they
shout the destination of their long-haul carriers. Small boys act
as touts for the bus companies and rush through the throng
shouting a single name: 'Denizli, Denizli, Denizli . . .' (We
never discovered quite where Denizli was, but imagined a
sort of spaghetti junction in the middle of Asia Minor with
nocturnal juggernauts roaring through it.)

Erzurum bus depot was calmer and we made our reconnaissance in daylight. It seemed impossible to reach Lake Van without interminable changes and spending nights at places where, we suspected, there was nowhere to spend the night, except perhaps some latter-day *han*. Eventually we found a driver who professed to be leaving at ten at night for Ahlât, on the northern shores of Lake Van. This was on our itinerary, as we knew that Tamerlane had passed through Ahlât on this campaign, and from there we knew we could get on to Tatvan and Van itself – even more important places from Tamerlane's point of view – on the southern shores of the lake. Only when we had paid for our 'tickets' (a dirty scrap of paper torn from an exercise book) did we discover that his bus was, in fact, a lorry. It was too late for backsliding: we decided that the only sensible course was to eat and drink so much during our remaining hours in Erzurum that we would slumber away the night on the road. We ate a strange type of waffle, drenched in the wild 'mad' honey for which the region has been famous since the days of Xenophon; we indulged in strange beverages which – although served to us by Muslims in a Muslim country – seemed to induce a curiously muzzy effect, which, in other circumstances, we would have attributed to alcohol; we reached the bus depot in a state recognized in military circles throughout the world as 'not feeling much pain'.

It was well that it was so. When we reached the prearranged departure point for our lorry, it had long been dark. There were two other passengers: an Armenian merchant and his wife were returning to Van with some carpets which they had bought. We were surprised to encounter Armenians, as we had understood that ever since the persecutions early in this century there had been few of them in evidence in this part of the country. It was clear that we were all expected to travel in the back together. The floor of the lorry was full of sacks of grain. The Armenians knew how to make themselves comfortable and pulled and pushed the sacks till they had created little furrows; into these they slotted themselves and covered everything with the carpets. These were not the usual garish rugs to be seen in the Erzurum shops nor the primitive tribal rugs with their simple but engaging designs: they were Sivas carpets brought from the heart of Anatolia, but the motifs were clearly of Persian inspiration, and bore some resemblance to Tabriz carpets in their central medallion, floral decoration and occasional animal motifs. What distinguished these Sivas carpets particularly was the high density of their knots, the ivory colour of the backgrounds and the soft pastel shades of the patterns. They were gentle, sophisticated carpets for rich men's houses, not the bold geometric rugs in primary colours to which we had become accustomed near the Qarabagh and which we were to encounter again with the Qashqai in southern Persia. The Armenians explained that their wares had all been produced before 1920; since then, they said, the volume of production at Sivas had increased but the quality declined. They offered us a share of the carpets for the night; seldom had we been wrapped up in such warm and decorative bundles.

The night that followed seemed unreal at the time, and now I find it hard to recollect any distinct impressions at all. It may have been the honey, or the cold – which became quite intense despite the carpets – or the jolting motion of the lorry, or the ceaseless z-bends as the road climbed and descended everrecurring ranges. We were neither asleep nor awake. The lights of the villages through which we trundled came from nowhere and were lost as quickly in the ensuing darkness. Even our halts at village *hans*, where we jumped stiffly off the lorry to down hot glasses of sweet tea . . . even these have blurred beyond recall.

Chapter 9

Tigris and Euphrates

The next day was far spent before we reached Ahlât, but I shall never forget our first glimpse of Lake Van. I had been warned of its size (which is more than six times that of Lake Geneva) but I had not been prepared for its brilliant, almost metallic, blue colour. This is due to the fact that the water is highly alkaline, a feature which gives it other interesting characteristics too. The inhabitants of Ahlât and other lake-side settlements claim that they can wash their clothes merely by swishing them round in the soda-laden water. Certainly, we saw numbers of women apparently doing just this. Bathers, too, find the qualities of the water unusual: we were to emerge from swimming feeling as if our skins had acquired a silky texture, but with an unpleasant taste in our mouths. But if the accounts given to Captain Burnaby in 1876 were to be believed, bathing could have unusual hazards: he was told that the springs were so hot that 'a man could not put his hand into the water without being scalded'. Fish, presumably apprehensive of being boiled before their time, shun the body of the lake and are only to be found in the fresher waters where rivers flow into it. Looking across the lake and studying the distances on the map, as best I could in the jolting lorry, I was surprised at how well I could see the southern shore, until I realized that the mountains at which I was looking were mostly over 9,000 feet.

The castle of Ahlât, of which the extensive walls still stand along the lake-side two miles west of the town, is not the one which Tamerlane stormed and captured. It was mostly constructed by Kanuni Sultan Suleyman in the sixteenth century, but it is believed to be on the site of the earlier castle; geography suggests that this is likely. When we arrived there, an old woman was scratching about among the ruins and produced some ancient coins, so worn that the inscriptions were indecipherable to the unpractised eye, from the voluminous folds of her skirt. We bought one for a small sum to cheer her up, but doubted if numismatic circles in Istanbul would be very excited by our find.

As with so many places along our trail, the most interesting feature of Ahlât today is the same as in Tamerlane's time. In this case it is the *turbes* dating from the end of the thirteenth century. *Turbes* were to the Seljuk dynasty what pyramids were to the ancient Egyptians: at one and the same time, a tomb and an art form. We had seen *turbes* of a similar description in Erzurum, and indeed they are a feature of Eastern Anatolia. There is a theory that the shape of the *turbe* is modelled on a tent or a Mongol *yurt*, but to us they looked like large pepper-pots, standing usually some ten feet high, with cylindrical sides and a conical roof. The body of the departed would in some cases be suspended upright in the shaft of the *turbe*, but more generally be buried below. The exterior might be plain, or elaborately carved stone, depending on the wealth and status of the occupant. Many of those at Ahlât have been much restored, but the famous Buğatay Ağa Türbesi and the Hasan Timur Ağa Türbesi which were built in 1280 are still a superb blend of delicate carving and austere design.

We wandered for a while among these strange pepper-pots which had resisted the ravages of Tamerlane as successfully as they had those of subsequent waves of invaders. The wind across the lake ruffled the tall grass. Suddenly we felt exhausted after our long night of lorry travel, and we lay down and dreamt of Tartars riding through the long grass and plunging their horses into the waters of the blue lake. When we woke the old lady with the coins was sitting watching over us like some kindly genius of the place.

We caught the once-a-day bus in the evening into Tatvan, a small modern-looking town which stands at the south-western corner of Lake Van. Here there were no traces of Tamerlane or his Seljuk predecessors, but many reminders of more recent Russian occupation; some people even said that the unprepossessing villas built along the edge of the lake dated from that period. There was also an hotel, where we found an adequate room and a telephone.

This last was, for the first time since our trip had started, one of our requirements, since we had an introduction to the military commander of the region which ran from Diyarbakir in the west to Van in the east. We had seized on the introduction when it was offered to us by a Turkish ambassador of our acquaintance, because we recalled how significant letters of introduction had been to previous travellers in the region; we remembered the Rev. Joseph Wolff sewing letters to the Emir of Bukhara into his clerical coat, and poor Stoddart and Conolly ending up in the same Emir's snake pit because they lacked adequate letters. We thought that if we followed up our introduction we might find access easier to some of the more remote places we wanted to visit. Grappling with foreign telephone exchanges and military switchboards is never easy, but our efforts were rewarded beyond our wildest expectations.

The General said he would not only do everything to smooth our path, he would send a staff car and driver to take us wherever we wished as long as we were in his Region. The driver would report to us at ten o'clock the following morning. This was luxury indeed to two travellers whose idea of speed had become a local bus, and of comfort a mule saddle. Better still, it extended our range.

We went out to look for dinner in Tatvan in a celebratory mood, talking of ordering a bottle of wine to toast our luck. We were quickly brought back to reality. Whatever curious drinks might have been available at Erzurum, wine or any form of alcohol was apparently unobtainable in the Muslim ambience of Tatvan; and Caroline's presence in the restaurant was clearly viewed as an embarrassing lapse of propriety. We were hustled through a cheerful room crowded with men into a poky back parlour across the doorway of which a bead curtain was hastily drawn to protect the good men of Tatvan from female distractions over their food.

Over dinner we discussed the new horizons opened to us by a car and a military escort. Hitherto we had thought of rounding Lake Van to Van itself and then striking south-eastwards to recross the Iranian frontier near Essendere. Now we could contemplate making a further stab into Anatolia as Tamerlane's own advance columns had done before they had rejoined the main body of his army to consolidate their position round Van. The furthest point into Turkey which Tamerlane's vanguard had reached was probably the mountains west of Diyarbakir. The latter was – and is – a walled city standing on the banks of the Tigris and commanding the undulating countryside around. For seventy-five miles to the west of it lies the fertile region between the Tigris and Euphrates valleys; but thereafter the mountains rise steeply and it seems likely that Tamerlane felt this was as far as it was expedient to probe on his first Turkish campaign. We would go this far also.

And it so happens that at approximately the point where he must have turned, there lies one of the most curious archaeological sites in all Turkey: the terraces of giant heads carved out of rock by Antiochus I on the summit of the mountain of Nemrut Dağ. These had been there since approximately the year 40 B.C. Whether Tamerlane had seen them we would never know, but they would be our next objective and turning point.

We might have slept in the following morning, but this is a difficult thing to do in eastern Turkey. Life starts at first light, and well before 6 a.m. every little town is bustling with activity. Tatvan was no exception. We got back to the hotel after a morning walk along the shore of Lake Van, to find our military driver – Ahmet – and a black saloon car already waiting for us. Ahmet was not in uniform but wore a well-pressed shirt and trousers and highly polished black shoes. We explained our plans to him with the help of the local garage owner, and he seemed to enter into the spirit of them. We set off immediately for Bitlis, the first stage of the day's drive to Diyarbakir.

The road leaving Lake Van for the west is mountainous for the first twenty miles. We had been warned by official sources before leaving London that this was a dangerous part of the country: 'robbery is endemic and night travel should not be considered', the messages had said. Ahmet made the same point more vividly as soon as we left the last habitations of Tatvan behind us: he fumbled in the glove compartment of the car and produced an ancient Lüger which he laid quietly and without comment on the shelf in front of him.

Armed guards have ever been a feature of this part of what was formerly known as Turkish Armenia. At the end of the last century Wratislaw had found it necessary to have his carriage escorted by two gendarmes armed with Winchester rifles 'of an ancient pattern evolved in the American Civil War more than twenty years before, and using rim-fire cartridges'. He goes on to say: 'I had the curiosity to examine the bandolier of one of them and discovered from the tell-tale indentation in the rim that two-thirds of them had already missed fire.' I felt I would not have liked to subject the Lüger to similar scrutiny: it looked more than twenty years old to me, and I suspected that it had won its spurs in the First rather than the Second World War when the Turks – as allies of the Germans – must have been in receipt of many such small arms.

The dangers of this route have never deterred travellers; we were now on one of the world's great caravan roads, and the proof of this was soon evident in the appearance of caravanserais at irregular intervals. These are unmistakable and highly practical buildings: they appear like square forts from outside with unadorned high walls only relieved in most cases by ornamental central gateways, sometimes surmounted by a square tower. Occasionally there are also corner turrets. Inside, there is usually a pillared arcade running round an open quadrangle (though in Turkey this is not as uniformly the case as in Persia).

It is here that travellers would spend their nights, with their caravans of animals and baggage. The horses, camels and mules would be tethered in the stabling provided by the arcade, while the travellers themselves would sleep in rooms behind or above. Slightly grander rooms would sometimes be available in the gate tower, but more often this would be occupied by guards who were the permanent staff of the caravanserai and whose job it was to bolt and chain the heavy gate at night, and defend the lodgers against the bands of robbers for which the region was – and by some accounts still is – renowned.

On the road to Bitlis we passed one well-preserved but disused caravanserai, and on entering the little town found another of unusually fine design, with a carved portal. This had been built in the sixteenth century, but not a few of them were of much earlier construction.

Tamerlane himself had paid great attention to the safety of travellers on the main roads within his empire. It has already been noted that nothing more surely brought down his wrath than the harassment of pilgrims and traders on the highway. The imperial couriers were particularly privileged. Clavijo records that at regular stages on his journey across the empire, from Trebizond to Samarkand, there were stables full of swift mounts held in waiting for the couriers. If, by chance, the courier's horse collapsed or went lame, then he had the right to requisition any substitute horse he could find, even if it were the favourite stallion of a prince of the blood, or the charger of the local garrison commander. Mindful of their powers, these messengers bullied unmercifully all whose services they required. Clavijo describes how on entering a village they would seize the first man they saw and, tying him to a stirrup by his turban, force him to bring them to the local headman, who would then be 'beaten with wondrous vigour' as a prelude to being confronted with demands for fodder and refreshments. It was little wonder that Persian villagers rushed to shutter up their shops at the approach of Tamerlane's emissaries. The messengers were all-powerful: the dispatches had to get through.

This priority was not surprising. Tamerlane, like Napoleon after him, ran his empire from his campaign tent. Just as the Marquis de Caulaincourt, Napoleon's aide and ambassador, organized a system of dispatch riders across the empire that enabled Napoleon to continue to run the affairs of Paris from Moscow (the delivery time for his mail was eight days), so

Tamerlane continued to run the affairs of Samarkand, Bukhara, Isfahan and Tabrīz from Lake Van or wherever his campaign might take him. And he was not only deciding matters of grand strategy and high policy: he was approving the designs for mosques and palaces; ratifying or reversing the judgements of provincial governors, and embarking on exchanges of diplomatic insults and challenges with a wide variety of sovereign rulers.

The caravanserai was not the only attraction of Bitlis. The situation of the town itself is remarkable, being in a narrow gorge which restricts the total width of the town at its narrowest point to a rapidly tumbling river, a narrow road and two rows of yellow stone and wooden houses. The mixture of stone and wood is brought about by the need to split up the stone sections with wooden 'courses' or beams, designed to act as shock-absorbers in the event of earthquakes. The fortress above the gorge dates originally from the time of Alexander the Great; nothing of the original walls remains, and the local legend attributes their destruction to Tamerlane. But although it has its share of ruins, Bitlis is by no means a sad place. Beside the river are tea-gardens and restaurants where the local population – or, more precisely, the male part of it – meets to talk and play backgammon (a game well beloved by Tamerlane). Ahmet disapproved of our loitering here and bustled us into the car; as the dust of Bitlis settled behind us, the Lüger reappeared.

The countryside became gentler and greener; we passed Baykan and Silvan, and saw numerous groups of Kurds moving cheerfully with their sheep and goats across the rolling uplands. One could spot them from a great distance, particularly the women, who wore bright multi-coloured skirts and blouses, topped with flowing white head-dresses which, in turn, were crowned with small gold pill-box caps. They looked totally innocent of the reputation for treachery and violence about which we were later to hear so much.

Some of the shepherds we saw were wearing drab coloured but unusually shaped coats – built out at the shoulders like those of Chicago gangsters of the 1930s. On closer inspection, the garments turned out not to be coats at all, but upturned fertilizer sacks in which a hole had been pierced for the wearer's head. They were undoubtedly a remarkably weatherproof, as well as remarkably economical, form of dress.

Had Tamerlane and his host been capable of feeling dread, the first sight of Diyarbakir would surely have induced it. Not only are the walls unusually high but they are constructed of sombre black basalt. Tamerlane was never one to bypass a difficult fortress or town; he disliked enemy enclaves in his rear. But even if he had been so inclined, he could not have bypassed Diyarbakir, because the town dominates a strategic ford on the Tigris. Walls overlooking a river: that is the essence of Diyarbakir.

We started on the walls. Ahmet knew a good point at which to scale these, and soon we had scrambled up to remarkably well-preserved battlements which seemed to provide nesting accommodation for every stork in Eastern Anatolia.

Next we went to have a closer look at the river. Atatürk had a summer residence at Diyarbakir, outside the walls and on the banks of the Tigris. Ahmed showed us proudly round the rooms of faded photographs: Atatürk in uniform and holding enormous binoculars at military manoeuvres in 1922; Atatürk in morning coat surrounded by railway officials at the opening of some new line to Ankara; Atatürk still looking remarkably formal in his gardens at Diyarbakir. He had ruled this part of the world as firmly and decisively as ever Tamerlane had done, but the contrast between the styles of the two men was even greater than the gap in time that divided them: Atatürk – dapper, organized, urban; Tamerlane – intemperate, flamboyant, a dweller in tents. I was still pondering on the contrasts when I heard Caroline, who has a more practical turn of mind, enquiring earnestly from Ahmet about where one could dine well in Diyarbakir.

The best restaurant, it appeared, was in our hotel; which in turn was the best hotel; which in turn was not saying very much. It mystifies me how the Turks and Persians can display such an amazing sense of colour harmony in their carpets, and such a total disregard of this faculty in their interior décor. Diyarbakir's answer to the Hilton had twelve rooms, three on each floor. Every floor and, we were assured, every room was painted a different colour, as was every wall in every passage and public room. Pastel shades had not yet come to Diyarbakir: puce and violet, electric blue and chrome yellow, mauve and peacock – these were the reigning favourites.

Having braved this kaleidoscope of colours, we reached the restaurant on the top floor. The Turkish custom of inviting diners to go into the kitchen and select their own food is doubly appreciated when one's grasp of the language is inadequate: an investigatory look and a pointing finger in the kitchen can obviate the need for much verbal enquiry and misunderstanding in the dining room.

As so often in Turkey, we were struck on this occasion by how one human activity is not allowed to hamper another. In the centre of the kitchen floor, the chef was saying his prayers. As he did not have a prayer mat, he had laid out a small drying-up towel on the tiled floor and it was on this that he was making his obeisances in the direction of Mecca. Skirting him with care, we reached the stew pots and found a selection of inviting-smelling pilaffs and mutton dishes. Negotiating our return to the dining room we had to circumvent the cashier, a rotund gentleman who was standing in the middle of a narrow passageway while a diminutive and obsequious tailor measured him for a new pair of trousers.

The meal was as good as it smelt in the kitchen. Although Caroline was the only woman in the dining room, she was neither asked to eat elsewhere nor made the subject of any particular attention; it was I who felt conspicuous when she pointed out that I was the only man in the room without a moustache. We asked for *baklava* as a pudding, but as this Turkish sweetmeat appeared not to be available we were brought a substitute which looked and tasted exactly like shredded-wheat cereal, soaked in honey and compressed. Perhaps it was.

The rest of our night at Diyarbakir was not so happy. The shower room off our bedroom was ankle deep in other people's dirty shower water, and worse. The ubiquitous slippers provided were inadequate vehicles of ferry to the loo. Mosquitoes and other biting insects either invaded our room, or – more likely – were the established residents and so felt entitled to prey on us as the interlopers. And we suffered from traffic noise: not, let me hasten to add, from motor vehicles but from horses and carts, which neighed and trundled respectively throughout the short night.

We were glad we had asked Ahmet to meet us at 5.30 a.m. Already the town was a bustle of activity and we knew we had a long day ahead, as we were attempting to reach Nemrut Dağ and return in one day.

The land between the Tigris (on whose banks we were at Diyarbakir) and the Euphrates (which runs at the foot of Nemrut Dağ) is universally known as the cradle of civilization.

In fact, the great civilizations of pre-biblical times were to be found far downstream of us, in the hotter, flatter plains of Mesopotamia. The country we traversed in Ahmet's car between 5.30 and 8 a.m. was green and rolling. This was not the land of Sodom and Gomorrah. The mighty Euphrates when we crossed it was not a broad, brown, matronly river suckling a parched land, but a bubbling, blue and almost sprightly torrent.

Kâhta was our stopping place. Here we had to abandon our military staff car since the local wisdom was that the road and track which approached the summit of Nemrut Dağ was repeatedly intersected at this time of the year by fast-flowing streams of melted snow coming off the mountains, and our only hope of passing was in a Land Rover. We spent an hour at Kâhta drinking endless cups of green tea while Ahmet negotiated the hire of a Land Rover for a princely sum. It may be that the inhabitants of Kâhta are honest, hard-working folk who were charging no more than the going rate in these parts. But their appearances are against them: everyone with whom we spoke had the most villainous squint and appeared to be looking over our shoulders, or at his neighbour, or both, while explaining to us the uniquely costly nature of the services we required.

When we were once more under way, we found our party was augmented by the owner of the Land Rover and his son. In one respect they had certainly been honest with us: the streams were indeed swollen and fast-flowing and Ahmet said that military regulations would not have allowed him to hazard the staff car on attempted crossings. We passed through two Kurdish villages at the first of which we bought a picnic from a village store which specialized in a strange variety of goods: bright coloured cloth, for making clothes for the locals; rope;

The Shahrestan bridge at Isfahan,
across which Tamerlane's army passed

Isfahan: city of domes and minarets

Persepolis – gateway to triumph

spices of bewildering variety; and – most improbably –
galoshes.

It was three hours from Kâhta to the point where the road
finally expired and where we abandoned our Land Rover. The
final stage was a simple quarter of an hour's clamber up stony
scree, spotted with wild tulips, to the snow-line. We crested a
ridge and saw at once the objective of our journey.

It seems that in approximately the year 40 B.C., Antiochus I
of the Kingdom of Commagene, who claimed descent from
both Darius the Great of Persia and Alexander the Great of
Macedonia, decided to attempt to invade heaven. He selected
the 8,000 foot peak of Nemrut Dağ as the most promising
jumping-off place, and constructed a huge pyramid of loose
stones on the summit. This he flanked with terraces of thirty-
foot-high figures of local deities, presumably to establish his
credentials. Earthquakes and the passing of twenty centuries
have toppled the figures, but their ten-foot-high heads remain
scattered over the terraces.

Some of the deities have the heads of monstrous birds, but
from the archaeologist's point of view the most interesting are
those in human form. They have the classical features of
Macedonian Greeks, but the head-dresses of Persian noblemen.
Antiochus's dual descent from Darius and Alexander is per-
petuated in these proud stone heads, which inevitably remind
one of Shelley's 'Ozymandias':

> Half sunk, a shattered visage lies, whose frown,
> And wrinkled lip, and sneer of cold command,
> Tell that its sculptor well those passions read
> Which yet survive, stamped on these lifeless things.

This was to be our furthest point west. It seems unlikely that even the advance columns of Tamerlane's horde reached further, and more probably they did not reach as far on this campaign. The conquest of central Turkey and the final destruction of Bayazid was to be postponed for a further five years until the mighty campaign of 1402 to 1404 immortalized in Marlowe's play. Even had Tamerlane's scouts crossed the Euphrates and mounted Nemrut Dağ, they would not have seen what we had seen. The terraces of heads were only excavated and set in order during the 1950s. Had Tamerlane found them, they might well have shared the fate of the great bronze gates of Bursa, which were transported from the shores of the Bosporus to Samarkand to grace the entrance to the conqueror's mother's tent. And even if Tamerlane's eye had rested on the proud stone heads, it seems doubtful if he would have drawn Shelley's conclusions about the ephemeral nature of power and glory. His was a defiant temperament which challenged not only man but destiny:

> I hold the Fates bound fast in iron chains,
> And with my hand turn Fortune's wheel about.

Far from being pensive, Tamerlane was about to commit an assault which, even for him, was unusually bold and bloody.

Chapter 10

Eastward from Lake Van

The penalty for having abandoned the route of Tamerlane's main army, and having taken the line of one of his probing columns instead, was that we now had to retrace our steps.

The Land Rover took us back to Kâhta, and Ahmet escorted us again – his Lüger ever at the ready – across the Euphrates to Diyarbakir. We spent another night among the violent hues and hungry insects of the hotel, and then went on across the Tigris and its numerous tributaries, through Bitlis to Tatvan again. Ahmet said he could take us on to Van itself, at the eastern end of the lake, as this town stood within the confines of his General's military region; so we now drove for the first time around the southern shores of that great expanse of bright water.

A few miles before we reached Van, we came in sight of Akhtamar Island and, as luck would have it, a small boat, loaded to the gunwales with voluble Turks, was just setting out in the evening sunshine for the short voyage to this holy island, famous for its tenth-century Armenian church. Ahmet persuaded the boatman that three more passengers would not materially increase his risk of sinking.

Although Tamerlane's columns might reasonably be assumed

to have missed the terraces at Nemrut Daǧ, they could not possibly have missed the church on Akhtamar Island. It is visible from the shore and, at the period in question, was flanked by a monastery which has since disappeared.

Tamerlane was no lover of Christian churches. In a later campaign at Erzincan (300 miles further west) he was to destroy the churches even after receiving a generous ransom for the safety of the Christian community. At Smyrna he not only destroyed the churches but used the heads of Christian knights as cannon balls to bombard Christian shipping. How then did it come about that, when Tamerlane was roaring destructively around the shores of Lake Van, he should have preserved this exquisite gem of Armenian architecture?

This was one of the questions we had in mind as we jumped ashore from the little boat on to the green turf of Akhtamar. No one now lives on the island and our crowded boatload was soon absorbed into the silence of the place. Caroline and I hopped over a lazy snake that lay sunning itself on the stone path to the church, and soon found ourselves staring at the richly carved walls, their bas-reliefs given enhanced contours by the shafts of evening sunlight that played softly on the golden stone. Here we could identify David and a seven-foot Goliath, Daniel in the lion's den and other biblical scenes.

The theory of how Tamerlane came to spare Akhtamar rests on the fact that Tamerlane did not really begin to hate Christians until later in his career – until, in fact, he felt that he had been deceived and betrayed by them. This was only to happen during his campaign of 1402 when he was fighting against the Sultan Bayazid of Turkey who was by that time threatening Constantinople. The Christian world was inclined to consider any enemy of Bayazid as an ally of theirs. Although Tamerlane was already known in Europe as a Muslim barbarian, envoys were none the less dispatched to him with a view to establishing some working alliance against the most immediate enemy – the Ottoman Turks. The Christian monarchs of Europe knew that they were playing with fire, and their overtures were doubtless made in the spirit in which Sir Winston Churchill, when accused of a sudden burst of friendliness towards Communist Russia in 1941, replied: 'If Hitler invaded Hell, I would at least make a favourable reference to the Devil in the House of Commons.' It was Bayazid, not Tamerlane, who was knocking at the gates of Christendom at the close of the fourteenth century (and, indeed, it was to the Turks and not to the Tartars that Constantinople was ultimately to fall in 1453). The Christians' treachery in Tamerlane's eyes consisted of allowing Turks to cross the Dardanelles in both directions: as refugees from Tamerlane and as reinforcements against him. Tamerlane rightly concluded that the Christian monarchs of Europe had been content to see him and Bayazid slaughter each other's forces on the plains of Asia Minor. He did not forgive.

But all this was in the future. As Tamerlane's hordes circled the shores of Lake Van and stumbled on the church at Akhtamar he was not inexorably committed to the destruction of all Christian places of worship. However, as we stood in the clear evening sunshine in front of the beautifully carved exterior of the little island church, it occurred to us that perhaps there was a more positive and personal reason for Tamerlane's having saved Akhtamar. Might not the clue lie in the carvings themselves? The subjects of these were not restricted to biblical scenes, but included representations of the chase: hares and foxes, stags and lions were all depicted, and even some of the religious subjects – notably the vignette of Samson killing a lion – had a distinctly sporting flavour. Could it have been that the passionate hunter of the Qarabagh looked on this church as a shrine to his favourite pastime and thus spared it for posterity?

We speculated on this as we re-embarked for the shore and as Ahmet drove us on the final lap of our journey into the little lake-side town of Van itself. It was too dark to see anything, but Ahmet found a small and reasonably clean hotel where – since it had no dining room – we got directions to a good and crowded restaurant, approached down a narrow alley full of carpet vendors. As we ate delicious shashlik we speculated, like small children on Christmas Eve, about what we would see when the sun rose in the morning over the limpid blue of the lake and over the most formidable fortress that Tamerlane captured during this whole campaign.

The Rock of Van, on which the castle sits, is between the little town and the shore of the lake. It is one and a half miles long and its rock faces vary from steep to sheer, depending from which side it is viewed. It is a natural fortress and has been used as such for more than two thousand years. The proof of this is the trilingual cuneiform inscription to be seen on some of the smooth stones which flank one of the staircases cut into the rock. The inscription, in Babylonian, Achaemenian Persian and Median, was engraved by order of the Persian monarch Xerxes in the fifth century B.C. Tamerlane is unlikely to have seen it; and he could certainly not have deciphered it. Had he been able to do so, however, even he might have been taken aback at the monumental arrogance of the author:

. . . the greatest of gods, who has created this earth, who has created that heaven, who has created mankind . . . has made Xerxes king, sole king of many kings, sole lord of many. I

that there was treachery within, or the battering rams may have breached the lower walls. At all events, the capture was not without heavy loss to the Tartars, and Tamerlane – vindictive as ever – rounded up those of the defenders who had not been cut down in the fighting, had them bound by the neck and arms and thrown down from the summit of the Rock; some accounts say into the lake below.

We contemplated with amazement this act of vengeance as we stood – somewhat apprehensively – at the edge of the sheer rock face nearest to the lake: amazement not only at the savagery of the act, but at its improbability. Either the lake must have come much closer to the Rock than it now does, or the chroniclers must have invented this particular enormity, or Tamerlane (as at Smyrna) must have shot his victims from cannons into the water. By no stretch of the imagination could one today *throw* a person from the Rock of Van into the lake.

It was here at Van, after the fall of the castle and the return of the scouting columns from Diyarbakir and further west, that Tamerlane received news which was to alter his plans radically. It has already been remarked how closely he kept in touch with the affairs of his empire while he was on campaign. During his marches through western Persia and eastern Turkey, he had been monitoring with particular attention developments in southern Persia. Here he had had a vassal king in the person of Shah Shuja Muzaffar who had come to rule over the regions of Yazd, Kirman, Isfahan and Shīrāz in 1357. Muzaffar was a sensitive and delicate man, a patron of the poet Hafiz and 'so torn by faintness that he could not endure fasting'. (The fact that he had seized his own father, had him thrown into a dungeon and there had his eyes put out, does not appear to have unduly dented his reputation as a gentle scholar.) At all events, Muzaffar was mortally afraid of Tamerlane. He wrote grovelling letters to him – acclaiming him as 'wise as Solomon and great as Alexander' – and made public prayers that no quarrel should arise between him and his professed overlord. Tamerlane was perfectly content, as well he might be, with this state of affairs.

But in 1384, two years before the start of Tamerlane's present campaign, Muzaffar had (in the words of Ibn Arabshah) seen 'the valet of death fold up and remove from him the carpet of hope': he had died. And before his death he had made the fatal error of appointing Tamerlane to act as executor of his will.

This was an open invitation to intervene in the estate of the dead king. Tamerlane was not slow to see the possibilities of milking the rich and prosperous cities of southern Persia of far greater loot than he had ever received as tribute from his vassal Muzaffar. But as the region in question was already nominally part of his own domains, he needed a pretext for despoiling it.

Muzaffar had compounded the unwisdom of his will by dividing his estate between a variety of sons, brothers and nephews: it was only a matter of time until they either fell out between themselves, or one or other of them gave Tamerlane the excuse for intervention. Tamerlane was, in any case, in no hurry, being much occupied for the three years following Muzaffar's death with the preparations for and the execution of his first multi-season campaign. But by the autumn of 1387, with Tokhtamish driven from Tabrīz and Armenia at his feet, Tamerlane summoned Zayn Al-Abidin, the son who had inherited Shīrāz, to make his personal submission to the conqueror at his camp on the shores of Lake Van.

Zayn Al-Abidin declined the invitation. Perhaps like his father he was overcome by faintness at the prospect of physical exertion, or perhaps – also like his father – he was overcome by fits of trembling at the thought of a personal encounter with

Tamerlane. Whatever the reason, he was awaited in vain at the Tartar camp.

This was the pretext Tamerlane needed. A vassal had ignored his summons. Retribution would be swift and sure. With the castles of Armenia and eastern Anatolia already either occupied by his garrisons or destroyed, there was no cause to delay. The Tartar horde struck its tents, loaded its camels and mules, mounted its horses and turned eastwards.

If we were to follow the trail of Tamerlane we too had to turn our faces eastwards and execute a broad sweep through Kurdistan and Luristan to reach Isfahan and Shīrāz, not by the trunk road from Tehrān and the north, but by the less frequented route from the west. The only crossing point on this southern sector of the frontier between Turkey and Iran was at Essendere. Ahmet could not take us there: the road was too stony for his staff car; it was outside his military region; the people were unfriendly; there was nowhere to buy petrol, and – this last with a decisive shrug – 'nobody goes to Essendere'.

When pressed, however, Ahmet conceded that there might be a local bus to Yüksekova, which was only a few kilometres away from the frontier. If we could get that far, we thought, we might prevail on someone to take us on from there. When we got to the bus depot at Van there was the usual bewildering assortment of information and misinformation: the one bus of the day had already left; a bus was leaving shortly for Yüksekova but was already full; would we not prefer a bus back to Erzurum? The scene was beginning to resemble Smyrna, and at any moment I expected to hear cries of 'Denizli, Denizli!'

Then, quite suddenly, as so often in Turkey, the problem was resolved. A bus was indeed departing shortly for Yüksekova; there were two free seats; they happened to be the front ones. My suspicious mind immediately jumped to the conclusion that Ahmet had exerted military influence on our behalf. But the fact that Ahmet had taken himself off for a coffee and on return was clearly unaware of the change in our fortunes, and the charming way that the two Turks (who had indeed given up their seats for us) insisted to Caroline that it suited them just as well to stay a little longer at Van ('Van for me very good place today'), finally persuaded me that what we had just witnessed was not an example of military muscle but of traditional Turkish consideration towards benighted foreigners.

A gold bar (a jumbo pack of Benson & Hedges) proved a happy leave-taking present for Ahmet, and soon the Rock of Van and the peacock blue lake were no longer more than specks in our driver's rear mirror. We passed the romantic ruins of the seventeenth-century castle of Hoşap – a reminder that this region remained a disputed border one for many centuries after Tamerlane. Thereafter the going became steep for the elderly bus, and the landscape stonier and bleaker than any we had yet seen in Turkey.

We stopped for lunch at Başkale. At least that is what we assumed a stop for an hour at 1 p.m. was intended for. The other passengers disappeared with bewildering speed into narrow passages or curtained doorways where presumably they had friends to refresh them. We were left blinking in the dusty road.

Although Başkale was marked quite large on our map, it is in reality a tiny village, but on the corner of its sleepy square we found a small eating place. Although most of our ordering was done, as usual, by pointing to dishes in the kitchen, a certain amount of consultation was involved, and for this we drew on our well-thumbed Turkish phrase book. This was passed admiringly from hand to hand. The *patron* and his other clientele (all, needless to say, men) tried their tongues out on such English phrases as 'Where are the ruins of your temple? 'Is the gratuity included in the bill?', 'Take me to the Britisł Consul'. (Though not a modern book, it was socially progres· sive and there was not a mention of postilions.) The *patron* wa⸱ clearly enjoying himself and found that we and our idiosyn-cratic literature were providing a source of entertainment for his customers. Could he keep the book? he asked. Although we might not realize it, he seemed to be telling us, Başkale was really a cosmopolitan centre of busy sophistication, where a *restaurateur* required to have half a dozen languages on the tip of his tongue. Why, only last year, he recalled, a foreigner had dropped in for lunch; or had it been the year before? And per-haps he had not been a *real* foreigner like us, but he had certainly come from a part of the country where people spoke very strangely. A pub-keeper had to be prepared for such eventu-alities, he implied. Finally, the book would be a cherished memento of Caroline, he concluded, with a gesture that seemed to link her, the tattered phrase book and the grubby section of his shirt that presumably covered his heart, in an inexorable bond of romantic memory.

The little phrase book had been a life-line for the past few weeks but, if all went well, we would be across the frontier into Iran (and Farsi-speaking Iran this time, not the Turkish-speaking north-western provinces) by nightfall. With a charity which involved a formidable element of faith and hope, Caroline passed over our one remaining chance of being taken to ruined temples or British Consuls until we had left Turkish soil.

From Başkale to Yüksekova the countryside became increas-ingly attractive. Enticing valleys, belonging to tiny tributaries of the Tigris, beckoned us on either hand. Had we had camping equipment we would have been tempted to disregard the

Embassy's prudent advice about not sleeping outside villages; and we would have been foolish indeed to have done so in this heartland of the Kurds, so close to the conjunction of Iraq, Turkey and Iran. As it was, we descended to Yüksekova in the early evening and, putting all such irresponsible thoughts out of our minds, immediately began enquiries about how we could get to the frontier at Essendere that night.

Nothing could have been easier. After a mere four glasses of tea a roguish-looking Kurd, accompanied by two ladies with gold brocade on their dresses and white muslin bound round their wrists like bandages, invited us to join him in the back of a pick-up truck leaving for the four-mile-distant frontier post. When we arrived there, courteous – and slightly sleepy – Turkish officials waved us through with a minimum of formality. We humped the pseudo-Guccis across the two-hundred-yard no-man's-land to the Iranian frontier post, feeling full of goodwill towards Turks and Turkey.

Our guide book told us that in 1965 there had been only five foreigners who had crossed from Turkey into Persia at this point, all the rest of the traffic having apparently used the northern crossing place at which we had entered. Essendere is undoubtedly more frequented now, although we could have been excused for not realizing it. As the shadows lengthened from the flagpole from which fluttered the proud lion and sun of Iran, not a whisper broke the silence of the evening. Our roguish Kurd, whose decorative ladies had been left behind on the Turkish side, was clearly elated. With total disregard of the dormant immigration and customs houses, he strode off with a cheerful wave to us, and what appeared to be his bedding roll under his arm.

He did not get far. My faith in the security of the empire of the Pahlavis was restored by a shout of '*Yok*' from a guardroom and the emergence first of a rifle barrel, then of the head and shoulders of a soldier, and finally of the rest of the gallant musketeer who appeared to be still buttoning himself into his uniform.

Once the personnel of the frontier station had been aroused, there seemed no end to the formalities they could devise to complicate our entry. After health authorities, exchange control forms, customs inspection, the usual passport complications ('Thank you, Mr Mvo') we eventually emerged on Iranian territory free to continue our journey – if we could. There was no transport of any kind at the frontier post apart from a couple of motor cycles belonging to officials. The nearest village was two or three miles away. Our friendly Kurd appeared like a genie out of a bottle and said he would happily accompany us on foot and carry our cases. As he seemed determined on this charitable course, we thanked him and set off *à trois* for the walk to the village of Seru.

We had not got more than a couple of hundred yards when there was frantic whistling behind us. The largest of the frontier policemen eased himself on to the more powerful of the motor bikes and – with a passable imitation of an American crime chase – roared all of the two hundred yards down the road in pursuit of us. It seemed that our kindly Kurd had not been entirely disinterested in his attentions. Unlike us, he had not passed through the customs and it seemed that by attaching himself to us as a voluntary porter he had hoped to make good his departure under our auspices. With a resigned shrug he handed over our suitcases and plodded back to the customs shed.

We were sorry to lose his services. The pseudo-Guccis got heavier as the sun sank lower, and we wondered what we would find in Seru when we got there. It was a nasty disappointment.

Seru was, in effect, just another police station; a few small dwellings and a tea-house completed the metropolis. There was no sign of anywhere to stay, nor of any means of getting away.

But the police looked after us. They set up deck chairs in their compound, sent to the tea-house for a relay of glasses of hot tea, and promised a ride on one of their vehicles (which was momentarily expected) into the town of Rezā'īyeh. It was two hours later, when the last of the daylight had long disappeared and the fourteenth glass of tea had been drunk, that the police car turned up.

We bundled in, together with most of the personnel of the police station, and set off on a two-hour drive of which I have only one clear and recurring recollection. That is of huge, fluffy white sheepdogs picked up in our headlights as they sprang from guarding their flocks to pursue us angrily along the road, until we were out of the zone of their own responsibilities. I should not have liked to have been a pedestrian prowler.

We reached Rezā'īyeh at midnight. It had been an eighteen-hour day of almost continual travel, and we treated ourselves to a European-standard hotel, deciding that whatever transport we might miss in consequence we would sleep in the following day.

When we woke we could see to the west the mountains of the Turkish frontier through which we had passed the previous day, and to the east there was flat country for several miles between the town and the lake of the same name. It was called Rezā'īyeh when we were there; it was formerly called Urmia, and is now Urmia again, because 'Rezā'īyeh' was in honour of Reza Shah, the founder of the house of Pahlavi, and a name no longer to be conjured with in these parts. The lake could hardly be more different from Lake Van: the surroundings are either flat or relatively gentle hills compared to the mighty peaks encircling Lake Van; in many places it is difficult to approach the water on account of salt flats; the hue of the blue is quite unlike that of Van. In every way we felt in a different country.

This impression was increased by a short shopping expedition. In Rezā'īyeh, the shops had a surprising number of familiar products: packets of Tide detergent and Uhu glue peered down at us from dusty shelves like old friends caught in an embarrassing situation. Similarly we were surprised to find a number of Christian churches alongside the mosques of this Muslim town; on closer inspection they were either Armenian or Nestorian and some had their own mission schools. Perhaps we should not have been so surprised; after all, Rezā'īyeh, under its traditional name of Urmia, is supposed in some legends to be the place from which the Three Wise Men set off on their quest for the new-born Christ. With its Christian connections and its familiar household products, Rezā'īyeh was trying to make us feel at home.

But we could not linger here any more than Tamerlane had done when he was hastening through on his way to sort out the troubles of his southern Persian domains. And, like him, we next had to pass through a part of Persia as wild, and traditionally as lawless, as anywhere including the Valley of the Assassins: the provinces of Kurdistan and Luristan.

Chapter 11

Across Kurdistan and Luristan

We wondered what Kurdistan and Luristan might have in store for us as we wandered round the bus station at Rezā'īyeh trying to find a way of reaching Isfahan by the most direct route across this vast sector of south-west Persia. At the very least, it would be two long days of bus travel, and Kermānshāh seemed the best place to aim at for spending the half-way night. There are many bus companies which operate long-distance carriers across Iran, and several which operate across more than one country; some of these employ modern air-conditioned coaches with well-sprung seats and reliable drivers. By this stage in our travels we knew the names of a number of such companies and generally attempted to seek them out. None of those we knew appeared to operate a service on the unfrequented 300 mile road from Rezā'īyeh to Kermānshāh. We took what was available and, not surprisingly, we found that on this journey across the heart of Kurdistan the majority of our fellow travellers were Kurds of fierce aspect.

The Kurds have a reputation for being predators in the wild countryside on both sides of the Persian and Turkish – as well as the Iraqi – frontiers. But if they have often been the originators of violence, they have as frequently been the victims of treachery. The rulers of Tabrīz in particular were adept at tricking the Kurdish leaders to their deaths. Mr Consul Wratislaw recounts how Nizam es Sultaneh in the early years of this century was much troubled by a Kurdish chief in the region through which we were now passing. He therefore invited him to Tabrīz, supporting his safe-conduct with a public oath sworn on the Koran that as long as he, Nizam, was above ground no harm should come to the Kurdish chief. Once the Kurd was safely in his power, he had a pit dug in the garden of the palace into which he descended and – being thus below ground – promptly ordered the arrest and execution of his Kurdish guest.

The story appeared to Wratislaw as a good illustration of Kurdish gullibility. But Wratislaw was no admirer of the race and wrote that 'the only good Kurd is, as far as my experience goes, a dead Kurd, and the extinction of the race would be a gain to humanity'. Even making allowance for the more robust expression of a less inhibited age, the sentiment seems somewhat extreme for a British consular officer. Certainly our own experience of Kurds, though sometimes alarming, never tempted us to such venom.

Major Millingen, the nineteenth-century author of *Wild Life amongst the Koords*, maintained that the Kurdish girls were as dangerous to encounter as the men. He recounts that 'fair bandits' would lure a traveller from his carriage 'with dances and fiery glances of irresistible power' and as soon as he had alighted strip him to 'that primitive state in which Adam was at one time'. Their dances would then become provocative to the point where the traveller would 'reciprocate their advances' and be promptly charged with having assaulted the girls; the penalty consisted of being 'pricked with thorns upon a very sensitive part of his person' and obliged to pay a heavy fine. Tangling with Kurds seemed a hazardous pastime.

The Kurds on our own bus were fine-looking tribesmen, wearing their distinctive knotted head-dress and some with long-handled knives protruding from sashes and folds of clothing around their waists. We had grown used to sharing vehicles with people whose mien was ferocious and who yet had shown no inclination to be pugnacious. Mr Wratislaw would have warned us that we should not too readily assume their passivity. He would have been right.

We had been on the road for some four hours, travelling through sparsely populated country of no great interest, interspersed with villages whose idea of refreshment was yogurt diluted with soda water and served in dirty Coca Cola bottles, and whose idea of decoration appeared to be hanging out long lines of decapitated hens along the roadside, when the fight started.

We never really got to the bottom of the cause. We had, as usual, declined the front seats offered to us in the bus and had taken up a more sheltered position in the middle of the vehicle. From here we saw – and felt – the driver slam on his brakes for no apparent reason, leave his seat, stride like an angry Tartar back down the bus, pick up an apparently innocuous passenger by the collar of his quilted coat, and shake him till his teeth rattled. The passenger, it seemed, was not without friends. Four of these, all burly Persians, seized the driver and held him off. At this the Kurdish element, in whose section of the bus we found ourselves, rose as a man to rally to the driver. Suddenly hands stretched out towards those knives which, a moment before, we had considered such dashing evidence of local colour. The somnolent charabanc was transformed into a scene from *Alibaba and the Forty Thieves*.

The moment of violence, when it came, was so rapid that we

never saw exactly what happened. At one moment there were two quarrelling factions, at the next there were two people on the floor of the bus: one was a Kurd being held down by most of his own party, and the other was a nondescript youth who had a nasty blood-stain oozing through his shirt at the shoulder. The sight of blood seemed, in fact, to sober the whole bus. There was a polarization to different ends of the vehicle: the Kurds muttering fiercely but combining to restrain their clansman (while one of them cleaned the offending knife on the seat of his trousers); and the other passengers surrounding and nearly suffocating their casualty. The wounded man sat up, surveyed his blood-stained shirt and fainted histrionically. His associates redoubled their attentions and effectively denied any fresh air to him at all.

Caroline had once upon a time received the sort of first-aid instruction thought appropriate for young ladies in Ireland: she knows how to tend people who have fallen off horses, who have been kicked by horses, who have been bitten by horses, and who are suffering from shock at what has just been said to them by their MFH. But neither the first-aid courses at the Irish pony club nor the ones at her Swiss finishing school had devoted much attention to repairing those struck down by daggers.

However, at this point Caroline decided that if no one else was going to be sensible, she would have to be. Clutching our water bottle in one hand and her sponge bag in the other, she unceremoniously forced a path between the factions and parted the group around the casualty. Never did an international Red Cross unit more effectively intervene between two belligerent armies. Kurds and Persians fell back as Caroline ripped the sleeve off the unconscious man and examined the wound. It was not serious, but messy. She bathed the area around the cut, tore up the loose sleeve and bandaged the upper part of his arm where the Kurd's knife had lacerated the flesh. The victim regained consciousness, decided that it had been a mistake to do so, and lay back with a sigh on the floor of the bus again.

Now that the tension had been relieved, recriminations began. It seemed that the originally assaulted passenger had been casting audible aspersions on the motoring skills and prowess of our driver; these had become intolerable to that conscientious operative, who had decided to deal with his critic in his own way. Now that the fight had subsided, the driver remained adamant that he would not move the vehicle another kilometre until the offensive passenger – who was not the wounded man – had been ejected. Indeed, he seemed to be explaining that he had held his righteous indignation at bay for some time until he was sure he had reached a stretch of countryside where the passenger was least likely to find alternative transport. The passenger and his friends refused to countenance his abandonment at a lonely roadside in Kurdistan with night fast falling; he would have his throat cut. This was a sentiment which the Kurdish element took amiss; no one was unsafe in Kurdistan and they were prepared to slit the throat of anyone who maintained otherwise.

Eventually calmer counsels prevailed. The offending commentator was persuaded to make no more remarks on the skills or ancestry of the driver and to sit at the back; and the driver was persuaded to resume his seat and put the bus in motion again. The casualty was propped up on a seat and ceased pretending that he had expired. The two warring factions sorted themselves out to occupy the front and back sections respectively, and we were left in an uncomfortable no-man's-land in the middle. In these tense conditions we duly arrived in the clear evening light at Kermānshāh.

Having dumped the pseudo-Guccis in a modest *pension*, we decided to use the remaining daylight to see the rock sculptures of Taq-i-Bustan, situated some three or four miles to the west of the town under the shadow of an impressive mountain. These carvings date from the Sassanian period, approximately the third to seventh centuries after Christ. The most fascinating of them are executed within a grotto which leads from a delightful little garden and ornamental pond. Tamerlane would have found them as enchanting – if he spared time to look at anything on his rapid march eastwards – as I fancy he must have done the bas-reliefs on Akhtamar church in Lake Van, because like the latter they are devoted to the chase. Here are portrayed in carved panels scenes which would have reminded the conqueror of his happiest days in the Qarabagh: stag hunts in a forest, boar hunts in a swamp, camel trains carrying off the bag of dead game, elephant floundering in the marshes . . . and presiding over it all a knightly figure with whom Tamerlane would doubtless have identified himself.

The following day we entered Luristan proper. Even Tamerlane, we knew, felt some apprehensions among these rust-coloured, rounded hills – compared by Freya Stark to the upturned hulks of old ships – and among these wild, unpredictable tribesmen of whom Lord Curzon wrote: 'A people without a history or a literature or even a tradition presents a phenomenon in the face of which science stands abashed.' Literature the people of Luristan may not have, but history and traditions they do. No corner of the Middle East is richer in ancient tombs divulging treasure and bronzes of incomparable quality. This is the ancient kingdom of the Medes, united with the Persians under Cyrus, and authors of that law 'that altereth not'.

Some of the side valleys of which we got glimpses from our

road were narrow, dark and altogether more mysterious than these rounded hills. They lay like serpents coiled in between the rust-coloured rocks. The best description of riding up one of them was written in his diary in 1850 by Arthur Kavanagh:

> We arrived at a sort of cleft or opening between two mountains, through which a stream flowed. . . . Most of the road was a series of stairs, or rather natural projections of solid bare rock, over five or six feet in height, up which the horses had to jump without anything to prevent them, if their feet slipped, from rolling into the valley beneath. Sometimes the path ran along the bottom of a ledge of rock higher than one's head, the track being sometimes not wider than half a foot, and sometimes where the stones were broken away the horses had to step from stone to stone, like crossing a ford on stepping-stones, the precipice beneath ending in a river.

The reader may wonder why Mr Kavanagh did not dismount and lead his horse over these hazardous stretches. The answer is that he could not dismount. Nor could he walk. Nor could he handle a horse's reins. Mr Kavanagh had been born without legs or arms; he was strapped to a chair-saddle or carried about in a basket. This did not prevent him from travelling widely in the Middle East as a young man, from riding to hounds in middle age, or from becoming an Irish Member of Parliament and a Privy Councillor in later life. Memories are long in Luristan. When A. T. Wilson made a crossing of Luristan in 1911 he was escorted by an ancient scribe who regaled him with reminiscences of Kavanagh whom he had also accompanied sixty years previously. But then, no one would easily forget Mr Kavanagh.

When Freya Stark was exploring Luristan in the 1930s, it was

still a land where the central government's writ did not run by
any means as a matter of course. She had equipped herself with
letters from local governors and augmented these by showing
the British Foreign Secretary's injunction in the front of her
passport and explaining that 'it was signed by the King of
England's vizier'. Even so, when travelling in 'that part of the
country where one is less frequently murdered', she had her
share of narrow squeaks: her tent was entered by an intruder;
her own guide told her that if she had had a weapon he would
have stolen it himself; and she nearly lost her water bottle to
an acquisitive policeman. The Lurs boasted to her that 'there is
no one like us for stealing in the world', and their performance
over the centuries has lent considerable substance to the claim.

Tamerlane had found it necessary, at the beginning of this
campaign in 1386, to spend some weeks ostensibly in punishing
the Lurs for harassing the pilgrim routes, and in practice ensuring that they knew what would befall them if they interfered
with his own lines of communication. These punitive raids had
not only been an investment of time, but also of lives he could
ill spare. One of his imams died of wounds inflicted by the
Lurs, and three of his emirs succumbed to 'the intemperate air'.
A suitable number of captives were cast over mountain precipices to avenge these losses.

We were soon to have our own evidence of the fact that
memories are long in Luristan. When our bus made a diversion
off the road for some unknown reason (what hazards ahead
could have been worse than the rough going we were en-
countering?) we stopped at a wayside hut for yogurts and were
told that we were in the heart of the region dominated in the
1920s by a robber baron as bold as any who had faced Tamerlane – Mir Ali Khan. He had held sway from the fort at
Alishtar where he had installed himself and his five wives with

half a million *tomauns* in gold. The Lurs had loved him. He had fed three hundred of them daily at his table, and encouraged the regional sport of plundering and robbing representatives of central authority, until 'the plainsmen dared not sleep without their city walls'.

Affable as were our companions, I recalled Freya Stark's warning that hospitality and plunder have never been incompatible to Lurs. They would not let her pay for her lodging, but attempted to rifle her luggage. They would not let us pay for our drinks, but I noticed that Caroline was being edged further and further from her camera. Freya Stark had to sleep on her clothes; I made Caroline sit on her camera case.

Our principle when travelling by bus, particularly in Luristan, was to see our pseudo-Guccis safely into the luggage hold under the bus, and then to keep whatever we needed for the journey in our hands. Money was in any case secreted in a money-belt round my waist. (In Luristan they tell you that in Armenia they cut off your finger to get your ring, in Kurdistan they cut off your wrist to get your watch, and in Luristan they cut you in half to get your money-belt. There are still shades of 'there is no one like us for stealing in the world'!) The trouble with this plan was that when we came to retrieve our cases at the end of the day, Signor Gucci's bright coloured stripes had disappeared under a quarter-inch layer of congealed dust and all our clothes looked and felt as if they had been in a concrete mixer. But at least they were still there.

Not everyone was so lucky. In Isfahan we were to meet a young Australian couple who had attempted to cross Luristan but had got no further than the first village. There they had left their packs on the upstairs window-sill of a tea-house while they refreshed themselves as the guests of the local Lurs. When they came to buckle on their packs they were disturbed at how heavy they were and thought they must be more tired than they had realized. Only at the next stop, when they opened the packs, did they find them entirely full of rocks, wrapped in old rags, while no trace remained of their own clothes, food or films. Some light-fingered Lur had climbed up the outside of the tea-house, split the packs open, changed the contents and sewn them up again. The Australians should not have been surprised: the Lurs have had a formidable reputation for scaling walls since the time of the Crusades, when Saladin used them as the first wave of his assault on Christian castles.

Indeed, almost everyone who had crossed Luristan had his own stories of the ingenuity with which the Lurs would part travellers from their possessions. Isabella Bishop, a middle-aged widow who passed this way in 1890 – forty years after Kavanagh and forty years before Freya Stark – was one of the earliest recorded English victims. Mrs Bishop had spent the first half of her life as a semi-invalid, her most strenuous activity being a little local charity work. Then 'to improve her health' she had taken off on her travels. Having buried a husband who was ten years her junior, she made a tour of mission stations in Tibet and Kashmir and subsequently set off for home by a most circuitous route which took her eventually across Luristan. It was – predictably – on this leg of her journey that she was robbed. The thief who came to her tent in the night took, among other things, her cork sun helmet, her gloves, her sun umbrella, her thimble, her mask and her revolver case. The list conjures up an engaging vision of the lady's accoutrements. But it was not the loss of any of these which really upset her: the tragedy was that her embroidery had gone, and now she had no way of relieving 'the tedium of the long wait during the pitching of my tent'. In future she decided 'to rope the table and chair, on which I put my few remaining things, to the bed, taking care to put a tin can with a knife in it on the very edge of the table, so that if the things are tampered with the clatter may awake me'.

In the face of all this, we felt, what was a little dust in our suitcases as the price for crossing Luristan intact?

Chapter 12

Isfahan: Massacres and Monuments

Isfahan takes the traveller by surprise: situated in a region of stony desolation punctuated by improbable round pigeon towers, it rises like a mirage of domes and minarets, palms and fruit trees. Even in the fourteenth century – before the golden age of Isfahan – there must have been much to make the Tartar army gasp as they sighted their rich prize after the long dry marches across Luristan. The town was described by Mustawfi as 'full of excellent men and nobles . . . having always cheap grain and delicate fruits . . . and cattle fattened twice as well as elsewhere'.

Tamerlane pitched camp and drew up his forces in full view of the city. The thin November sunshine must have glinted on the dusty steel of helmets and spears; the still air would have carried the sound of drum and trumpet to the ears of the prosperous and comfortable citizens of Isfahan. The governor and elders met in conclave and quickly resolved to offer instant submission: a delegation was dispatched to the Tartar camp bearing the keys of the city and a suitably subservient invitation to take possession of their metropolis.

Although some elements of the Tartar army doubtless regretted the lost opportunity for rape and plunder, Tamerlane himself was gratified by the response: he made a triumphal entry, installed his own governor and garrison and set about confiscating horses and weapons, and securing the city gates and other key positions in his own hands. He rode back to his camp, taking with him the city elders as guests – and hostages.

And then the serious business of the day began: the negotiation of a levy for the protection of the city by Tamerlane's army – in fact, the dictation by Tamerlane of the ransom money he would accept as the price of denying his troops the sacking of the city. Despite the total absence of resistance, and the hero's welcome he had received, Tamerlane was as grasping as ever: he demanded a sum which amounted to almost the entire wealth of the city. With the Tartar garrison already in control, argument was futile. Nothing remained but to divide the city into tax collection areas, each presided over by one of Tamerlane's emirs supported by a body of Tartars, some three thousand strong in all.

The events of the following night have always been obscured by controversy, and the passing of six centuries has done little to clarify them. The inhabitants of Isfahan maintained that during the night the Tartar soldiery in the city became drunken, lecherous and unruly: brawls ensued in which both sides suffered casualties. The Tartars maintained that at a given signal –a drum beaten by a blacksmith – the supposedly innocent civilian population rose to a man and started murdering the garrison and the tax collectors. Whether they brought it on themselves or not, the fact is that very few of the three thousand garrison survived the night, and morning found the city gates in the hands of the burghers once more, who were busy defending them against the expected wrath of Tamerlane and his army encamped without the walls.

Apprehensive the townsmen might have been, but they could hardly have anticipated the terrible retribution that awaited them. Tamerlane's temper – never a predictable commodity – erupted in all its primeval fury. Arabshah caught something of the flavour of it when he recorded: 'When Tamerlane learnt of this evil crime, Satan puffed up his nostrils and he forthwith moved his camp and drew the sword of his wrath and took arrows from the quiver of his tyranny and advanced to the city, rearing, overthrowing, like a lion or dog or leopard.'

There was no time lost: before even the infamous black pennants had been displayed, a general assault was ordered. The city quickly fell to the enraged and savage Tartar assailants. The punishment, for what appeared to Tamerlane to be a gross act of treachery, was to be the execution of the entire population of Isfahan – men, women and children. The city elders, whose presence in the Tartar camp cleared them of any responsibility for the events of the night, alone were spared.

Just as the previous day the emirs had organized the city into zones for tax collection, so now they organized it for a more sinister toll. Units of the Tartar army were quartered in the different areas and each was ordered to collect a prescribed number of heads of the population. Even among the hardened campaigners of the Tartar horde, there were some who had scruples about slaughtering fellow Muslims in cold blood; these bought their quota of heads from their fellows in arms who had less compunction. The chroniclers record that the price of heads fluctuated from area to area and from hour to hour, ranging from half a kebek dinar to twenty kebek dinars. Even the fates seemed against the unhappy citizens: during the night after the massacre there was the unusual occurrence of a fall of snow in the city, and some of those who had eluded the execution squads were traced by their footprints and decapitated like the rest

When the bloody work was completed some seventy thousand heads had been counted by the emirs. They were piled outside the city walls and eventually, with the addition of mortar, built into minarets – as at Khvoy – as a monument and warning to any who might contemplate treachery against their Tartar overlords.

But despite all this slaughter, the structure of Isfahan had been very little damaged: the theory that nowhere which had been sacked by Tamerlane was ever the same again is not altogether borne out by Isfahan. Of course, the most celebrated glories of Isfahan date from two and a half centuries later – the period of Shah Abbas in the early days of the seventeenth century. It is from that period, too, that the famous pigeon towers date. These sprang up around Isfahan as an adjunct of the melon crop, for which the droppings of the pigeons were a much sought-after fertilizer. The towers themselves became a status symbol among local landowners – not unlike the *pigeonniers* found beside French châteaux – and sometimes rose to forty feet, giving a false impression of fortification to the approaches to the city. But even without its later glories and its pigeon towers, Isfahan had much to commend it architecturally at the end of the fourteenth century, and of this a significant amount remains.

Most notable of these surviving monuments of an earlier period is the Friday Mosque which was begun, in its present form, in about 1080 with the construction of the south dome chamber by the vizier of one of the Seljuk kings. Eight years later, the vizier's rival was busy constructing a north dome chamber expressly to outshine the other. After a fire, further construction continued under the Seljuk, Timurid, Safavid and

A mullah who befriended us at Shirāz

Qashqai in camp

The Khoda Khaneh, built by the Mongols a few years before Tamerlane's arrival at Shir.

Qajar dynasties. The mighty Tamerlane had left no direct trace here either of destruction or construction, since the Timurid winter prayer hall dates not from his own lifetime but from that of his descendant, Shah Rukh.

The one ancient monument that remains in Isfahan much as Tamerlane would have seen it is the Shahrestan bridge, a few miles to the south-east of the city. 'The piers,' Sir Roger Stevens tells us, 'are Sassanian, the pointed arches probably Seljuk.' Above the piers are smaller arches clearly designed to let flood waters pass through; these are thought to be Roman. Both the bridge and its setting – a shady road known as the Passage to Paradise and a backcloth of gaunt mountains – evoke a sense of timelessness. We sat by the fortified tower at one end of the bridge, Caroline waiting (unhappily in vain) for a camel train to pass over the ancient arches and provide her with the photograph she wanted, and I trying to visualize how the Shahrestan bridge must have looked on that evening in 1387 when Tamerlane and his army, their loot piled high on their ponies and camels and the blood of 70,000 Isfahanis still staining their hands and boots, lumbered across the Zaindeh river and headed towards Persepolis.

We were thinking about what other traces of Tamerlane we might find here as we studied town plans over our coffee in the hotel lounge that evening after dinner. Suddenly somebody walked into Caroline's chair, causing her to spill her coffee all over the map. I looked around crossly and was met by profound apologies from an elderly American with a deep southern accent.

'I'm so sorry, ma'am. Have I broken anything? I'm not seeing too well these days.'

Senator Abraham Hyam (which was not his name, but will serve as well as any other for the purpose) was a master of the understatement. It is doubtful if he would have passed the eye-sight test at a geriatric home for bats. We steered him into an armchair as he was about to sit down on the coffee tray, and put a cup into his hands. He produced a crocodile-skin cigar case – 'Do you young people ever care for a smoke?' – and then went on to tell us about himself with endearing candour. He was on an 'orientation trip' to Tehrān but had decided that he could not leave Iran without visiting Isfahan. Now he was finding it rather difficult to get around.

'Mrs Hyam's my eyes these days, and my eyes are right there under a hair-drier at the Tehrān Hilton just now.'

When we had gone back to our room and were preparing for bed, Caroline said, 'Poor Mr Hyam won't know whether he's in a mosque or a motel tomorrow. In fact it's really not safe for him to be wandering round on his own like that. Don't you think we should take him with us when we explore the town tomorrow?'

So we telephoned the senator's room and suggested that we should join forces after breakfast for a sightseeing trip.

'That's the best suggestion I've heard since my broker put me into Poseidon, ma'am.' We were committed.

The senator had decided that Isfahan warranted some sartorial effort. He appeared at breakfast clutching a ten-gallon stetson, and wearing a pale pink silk suit and wrap-round dark glasses which must have made it harder than ever for him to see any-thing. Perhaps catching Caroline looking at them, he said, 'They're fitted with special lenses. But don't you ever believe those tales about Texans having the windscreens of their auto-mobiles ground to their occulists' prescriptions. It's no good. I tried it. All that happened was that Mrs Hyam got one of her migraines every time we went any place.'

The golden age of construction in Isfahan was the reign of

Shah Abbas from 1587 to 1629. We decided to start our tour at the Ali Kapu palace on the Maidan. This is far from the most handsome of Isfahan's monuments; in fact, Robert Byron described it as 'that brick boot-box'. But it is the best vantage point from which to see many of the rest. The palace stands on the edge of the Maidan – that great open space which is the heart of Shah Abbas's Isfahan and which has at different times served as polo field, park, parade-ground and marketplace. It was from the high terrace of the Ali Kapu, with its tall wooden pillars and frescoes, that the Shahs watched the polo below; and it was from here that we pointed out the various sights to Mr Hyam. Possibly because it was the largest and easiest to see, he said he would like to go first to the Royal Mosque.

Sir Roger Stevens has described the Royal Mosque as 'the most majestic expression of Persian architecture at the crown of its most sumptuous and magnificent era'. Indeed, the Royal Mosque is a theatrical representation of Islam: the scale is vast, the tiling is brilliant blue, the whole is mirrored in ornamental water. This is the greatest opera set in Asia. The materials strive after effect rather than quality: the tiles are coloured but not mosaic; and the foundations are reputed to have started shifting within five years of the commencement of the work. We managed – in the nick of time – to head the senator off from walking into the *pièce d'eau*.

'Very glittery, very glittery indeed,' he said. 'A bit too much like walking about inside an enamel snuff-box for my liking. All this blue . . . all this blue. Mrs Hyam would be disappointed: she prefers pink.'

On this dismissive note we set out for fresh and more acceptable splendours. The Madrasseh-i-Shah is the last of the great buildings of Isfahan's golden age, and one of the loveliest. If there is a feeling of the theatre about the Royal Mosque, there is certainly a feeling of the cloister about the Madrasseh-i-Shah: the pruned trees, neat flower-beds and placid pools of the great courtyard remind one of a university college, which is essentially what this theological institution had been designed to be.

'It's as if Omar Khayyám had been asked to design Trinity Great Court,' said Caroline.

The senator did not agree that it was like a college campus. His attention had been arrested by the embossed silver door at the entrance portal: he kept returning to study it closely, and when finally we repassed it on our way out he turned with a sigh to Caroline and commented: 'I should really love to take something like that home with me, but Mrs Hyam would tell me there's too much cleaning involved.'

'Would you like to look for a present for Mrs Hyam?' asked Caroline brightly. 'We might go back to the Maidan and dive into the covered bazaar from there: there are fabulous carpets, and papier-mâché boxes made over a hundred years ago and painted with hunting scenes, and spices, and silver ornaments.' She made it sound like a veritable Aladdin's cave.

We looked at geometric tribal rugs from Shīrāz, and fine silk carpets from Nā'īn; we examined modern chemically-coloured products from Kermān and antique floral pieces from Kashan.

'They keep telling me about knots and motives,' Mr Hyam complained, 'when I've explained to them that it's the colour that's important to me. Red's no good. Orange is no good. All these blues are out of the question. If I've told them once I've told them a score of times, Mrs Hyam likes pink.'

Presents seemed too difficult. We lunched and completed our sightseeing with the Hakim and Sheikh Lutfullah mosques, and then set out in search of postcards to send to friends at home.

The sending of postcards takes up a totally disproportionate amount of the traveller's time and energy. First there is the choosing of the card itself; outside Europe the quality and degree of sophistication frequently leave so much to be desired that the effort to find anything which will not let down the sender's image can be exhausting. Blood-red sunsets over sailing ships may be all right for Aunt Mabel, but do little to inspire envy and awe in jet-setting contemporaries. Cheap facsimiles of illuminated manuscripts hardly hold their own on the crowded office mantelpiece of one's secretary. Unidentified sludge-coloured mosques will not be given pride of place around the edges of one's god-daughter's school looking-glass. The search for the right card is a gruelling one.

Then there is the problem of the text. The crisp witticism about the picture overleaf is all too likely to sound strained – or simply unintelligible – several weeks later and several thousand miles away. There is the disconcerting knowledge that informative remarks to one's nearest and dearest ('we're still hoping to be back on the 14th') are almost certain to be read after the event they forecast. One friend of mine had a simple message she transcribed on all cards from anywhere: 'Weather is here, wish you were lovely.' Whatever one writes is subjected to the hazards of perspiring hands, smudging biros and slopping wine on the café table before it reaches the pillar-box.

But to speak of pillar-boxes already is leaping over several arduous intermediate processes. It is almost unknown for postage stamps to be available where one buys the postcard. So a separate hunt for a *tabac* or equivalent is required. Local advice must be sought or guesses made as to the denomination of stamp required. Even when it has been purchased, one is lucky if the tiny oblong of paper has sufficient gum to stick to the card. The addressing of the card should be simple enough,

but the local version of England or Great Britain can well re-
quire looking up. Caroline had regularly despaired of learning
the Turkish for Great Britain and wrote cheerfully to her rela-
tions in 'Scotland, c/o Ingiltere'. They were not amused.

Now one is ready to hunt for the post-box. It is hard enough
in Asia to find one at all, and when one does it frequently has
that moribund, unvisited look that suggests a long sojourn for
one's missive before it starts its erratic journey. (When I read
references to 'dead letter boxes' in spy fiction, I always imagine
them looking like these Asiatic oubliettes.) It may be that I
have a suspicious mind, but I am loath to leave my carefully
selected and composed cards at any but the most convincing
hotel reception with the money for the stamps; I have an uncomfortable feeling that stamp money may be an accepted perk
of receptionists, and at some hotels I can think of I would not
be surprised to find the receptionist in a back room assiduously
steaming off stamps already affixed – before committing the
cards to the hotel incinerator. ('Your card didn't arrive, sir,
dear me . . . I'm afraid our postal service is sometimes a little
erratic . . . ho, ho.') I am a hoarder of cards until I find a
'promising' post-box. I know that others share my concern,
as I recently received a card from a friend which read: 'If this
ever reaches you, I shall have seriously misjudged the veracity
of the villainous-looking native who is encouraging me to slip
it into a crack in the rock which he improbably describes as a
pillar-box.' (That almost filled the whole space for text on the
card; I suspect he writes this on all his cards to save the effort of
further thought.)

Senator Hyam had applied himself with zest and determina-
tion to these problems: he had selected cards that would excite
envy in the hearts of his political associates; he had written
Texan witticisms on them; he had bargained about postal rates

with the porter at the Shah Abbas hotel, and expressed suitable scepticism about pillar-boxes. Finally, we had exchanged home addresses and promises to contact each other whenever we found ourselves in each other's countries. We were exhausted. Caroline and I found our way back to the peace of the Shahrestan bridge at sunset. The sun, like a golden ball, sank behind the mountains, illuminating the soft stone of the bridge with a roseate hue which in turn was reflected in the still waters of the Zaindeh Rud.

'What a pity he's not still with us,' said Caroline, 'Mrs Hyam likes pink.'

Chapter 13

In Triumph through Persepolis

Is it not passing brave to be a King,
And ride in triumph through Persepolis?

The best-known lines in all Marlowe's play associate Tamerlane indelibly with Persepolis. But in fact his connection with the great archaeological site was of the slenderest. He would have passed through Persepolis on his way across the Zagros hills between Isfahan and Shīrāz in the last days of 1387. It was already a ghost city with no burghers to meet him at its gates, no citizens to cringe at his glance, no coffers to offer up their spoils to his rapacious troops. Even in its heyday under Darius and Xerxes, Persepolis had never been anything but a seasonal abode for the royal court. The vast and magnificent terrace, at one time crowded with palaces, arches and processional ways, was never populated by any but the king and his harem, his court, their servants, guards and guests.

Darius had started the construction of the mighty terrace some years before he was defeated by the Greeks at Marathon, and his son Xerxes I continued the work in the intervals between his own defeats at the hands of the Greeks at Salamis, Plataea and Mycale. However unhappy their military experiences in the west, Darius and Xerxes were unshakeably established in strength and majesty here in the heart of their empire. But their successors were less secure, and it was during the reign of Darius III – the last of the Achaemenian kings of Persia – that Alexander the Great in 330 B.C. led his Macedonian army across the mountains and plains of Asia and occupied Persepolis itself. It will never be known for certain whether the terrible fire which largely destroyed Persepolis (more of the columns were of wood than of stone) was an accident or an act of incendiarism. Napoleon blamed Russian saboteurs for the burning of Moscow; Hitler would have liked to have left Paris in flames behind his withdrawal; Alexander is thought to have let Persepolis burn through carelessness.

But much remained. When Tamerlane rode up the one hundred and eleven gently graduated stone steps from the plain to the lofty gateway at the entrance to the royal terrace, he would have seen much of what we see today. He would have been able to trace, as the modern visitor can, the purposes of the different sections of the palace complex by observing the carved reliefs depicting the activities that took place on each particular spot. Thus the staircases up to the banqueting chambers portray servants bearing platters loaded with sweetmeats; the doorway to the private apartments portrays the king moving informally under a parasol; the audience chamber portrays him on his throne; the sleeping quarters portray eunuchs in attendance at the entrances. One can imagine Tamerlane pausing longest before the carvings on the great stairways, portraying processions passing up them: ninety-two warriors in Arab head-dress precede men carrying the royal dais and its surmounting throne; other warriors lead horses and chariots. Experts have identified tributaries from every corner of the Persian empire and beyond, bearing gifts for the sovereign: Egyptians and Babylonians with bulls; Bactrians with a double-humped camel; Arabs with dromedaries; Ethiopians, Ionians, Scythians and Parthians . . . all with their own tributes.

Could Tamerlane have drawn inspiration from these processional scenes for his own court at Samarkand? He had always attached importance to the outward and visible signs of respect from his vassals, and Marlowe was indulging in no more than a warrantable fantasy when he devised the famous scene in which Tamerlane is drawn in his chariot by the vanquished kings of Asia:

> Holla, ye pampered jades of Asia!
> What, can ye draw but twenty miles a day?

After his return from this campaign, he increased the ceremony of his capital and the frequency with which emissaries and satraps were summoned to pay their obeisances to the conqueror; all this was recorded by Clavijo when he reached his destination. When Tamerlane rode through Persepolis he was not only making a symbolic triumphal progress but was, in all probability, making mental notes for more impressive triumphs at home based on what he saw here. Marlowe makes his ideas on ceremony outshine even Darius:

> Then in my coach, like Saturn's royal son
> Mounted with shining chariot gilt with fire,
> And drawn with princely eagles through the path
> Pav'd with bright crystal and enchas'd with stars,
> When all the gods stand gazing at his pomp,
> So will I ride through Samarcanda streets.

Caroline and I also visited Persepolis on our way between

Isfahan and Shīrāz. We broke our journey and found we had
Persepolis almost to ourselves as we wandered among the
columns and massive blocks of stone, all reflecting the heat of
the midday sun. Never on all our journey had the heat seemed
so fierce, the shade so elusive, our thirst so oppressive or our
eyes so aggravated by dust. And this was spring – the time
of year when Darius and his court would have been in
residence.

But the day was not typical, as a sudden roll of thunder and
a downpour of rain declared. We wrapped up cameras and
notebooks and made our way to the nearby royal camp which
had been erected in 1971 for the celebrations of the 2,500th
anniversary of the foundation of the Persian monarchy. Only
the blue-striped tent-shaped pavilions remained to remind us
of that latter-day Field of the Cloth of Gold, when kings and
potentates from all over the world had assembled to join in
festivities which included *son et lumière* over the ruins of
Persepolis. Surely Tamerlane would have relished the occasion
as worthy of his own Zenocrate, to whom Marlowe makes him
vow:

> With milk-white harts upon an ivory sled
> Thou shalt be drawn amidst the frozen pools,
> And scale the icy mountains' lofty tops.

Our own thoughts were more plebeian and practical, mainly
centring on how we might complete our journey to Shīrāz
without waiting longer in the torrential rain. A small van,
which appeared to be acting as a freelance minibus, eventually
drew up and the driver indicated that he was returning to
Shīrāz and if we could squeeze into the front seat with him he
would take us for a small consideration. We packed in eagerly.

Among the imperfections of the van was a lack of wind-screen-wipers – a deficiency which on any occasion but the present would probably have worried the driver very little. However, the rain was now so heavy that the visibility – or rather the lack of it – was becoming positively alarming. Eventually the driver pulled in to the side of the road by a vegetable stall and bought a single onion. This he cut in two and used for wiping the windscreen, assuring us it was a sovereign remedy. The effect was far from convincing, but we set off at redoubled pace.

Caroline was the first to notice that whenever we passed a policeman, a police car or indeed anyone in uniform at all (which was a fairly frequent happening on the approaches to Shīrāz) our driver whipped out of his pocket a heavy pair of dark glasses and clapped these across his face. The result of this voluntary impairment of his vision, coupled with the now failing light, the heavy rain and the indifferent effects of the onion treatment, was alarming in the extreme. When we had nearly run into an ox-drawn wagon for the second time, Caroline pointed at the dark glasses and said firmly, 'No good.'

This evoked an excited harangue, which our all too apparent incapacity to understand did nothing to curtail. Nor was our confidence restored by a voice which emanated from under a pile of sacks in the back of the van.

'Driver say little accident better than big arrest.'

'Why should you be arrested?' asked Caroline.

'You really want to know?'

'No,' I said, 'we don't.'

There are moments when ignorance is an ally of innocence and I had decided that this was one of them. Soon we were entering the outskirts of Shīrāz and, no doubt sharpened by the recent rain, the scent of roses and herbs welcomed us to this city of fragrance.

In 1388 the citizens of Shīrāz had been watching events in Isfahan with anxiety tinged with panic. They decided to take no risk of being considered a foe of Tamerlane and, long before he reached their city of flowers and wine, they had started to arrange a suitably flattering reception for him: his name was included in the Friday prayer in all the mosques, and a camel was slaughtered as a peace offering. All Shīrāz was *en fête* for the conqueror's entry; and this time there were to be no mis-understandings.

The most renowned inhabitant of Shīrāz at this date was the poet Hafiz, whose verses were sung and quoted all over Islam and who had been invited as an honoured guest to courts as distant as India. Tamerlane himself did not read or write: as we have seen, there had been little time for acquiring such sub-sidiary skills during a boyhood spent learning the more im-perative requirements of archery and horsemanship. But he had developed and retained a taste for literature and intellectual activity: he commissioned the writing of verse accounts of his own campaigns and had them read aloud to him, and he played chess for hours – and even days – on end. He was therefore intrigued by the prospect of meeting the renowned Hafiz. There is a legend that Tamerlane summoned the old poet and taxed Hafiz with one couplet which had caused him offence; Hafiz in one of his wilder extravagances had written of his Shirazi lady love that he would 'give Bukhara for the mole upon her cheek, or Samarkand'. Tamerlane is alleged to have chided the poet with the fact that all the riches of Asia had been culled by his armies to beautify the cities of Samarkand and Bukhara, and here was a mere Persian poet denigrating such treasure houses and offering to swap them for the mole on a

Shirazi's cheek. Hafiz is said to have bowed profoundly before the conqueror and answered the charge by remarking: 'It is by such extravagance that I have fallen into my present impoverished condition.' Tamerlane was amused by the reply and showered gifts on the poet.

Indeed, Hafiz was fortunate not to have been sent back to Samarkand himself as were many of the most celebrated artists and craftsmen from Shīrāz. He remains buried in Shīrāz under a stone pergola in a tranquil garden punctuated by tall cypresses. We made this one of our first places of pilgrimage in Shīrāz and found it frequented by young Persian students who looked as if they might well be disciples of the great bard.

It may or may not be true that 'one is nearer God's heart in a garden than anywhere else on earth', but I think it is certainly true that one is nearer to the heart of Persia in a garden than anywhere else. Those who see only the bazaars and the bus stations forget that human over-activity nurtures a craving for calm; and those who see only the wild mountains and dusty deserts forget that the extravagances of nature breed a desire for containment. A Persian garden is the epitome of this calm and containment; there is a fragrance of herbs, a trilling of water, a quiet order in the trim paths, and a coolness in the pools of shade. Here in the garden of Hafiz at Shīrāz a boy played a pipe and it seemed to us that the music fell 'softer than blown roses on the grass'. This was the spiritual Persia which neither Alexander nor Genghis Khan, neither Tamerlane nor Reza Shah could destroy. As we watched the Persian youths strolling by with their books, learning their lessons by rote as they have done since time immemorial, we felt that after all it was Hafiz who had the last word, and perhaps his shy Shīrāz maiden really was worth more than all the power and splendour of Samarkand.

In our endeavours to see for ourselves the places Tamerlane
had known, we had visited many mosques in Persia; but few
as holy as the Friday mosque of Shīrāz. This shrine dated in
part from A.D. 894. But the building which was our particular
objective was the Khoda Khaneh, an imitation of the Khaba at
Mecca and built thirty years before Tamerlane's occupation of
the town.

On passing quietly through the main portal of the mosque,
we were accosted and stopped by a mullah carrying a long
staff. Clearly Caroline was not to be allowed to proceed, despite
the fact that her shoulders and arms were covered with an
ample scarf. Disappointed, we withdrew. We were not ten
yards from the gate when another mullah approached us and
drew us aside into an alcove off the gatehouse; here he presented Caroline with a black *chador* and indicated we should try
again to enter. This time we passed unremarked among the
throng in the outer courtyard, and made our way to a further
courtyard in which stood the celebrated Khoda Khaneh. It was
almost as if the Mongols had constructed a fortress within the
mosque: the Khoda Khaneh stood four-square, turreted and
uncompromising – an Islamic Ark of the Covenant. As in the
garden of Hafiz's tomb, so here, too, students passed up and
down, their lips moving as they learnt their lessons by rote.

We made an evening visit to the Vakil bazaar, a crowded
covered way where the brilliant colours of the tribal rugs are
only outshone by the garish hues of the Qashqai ladies' petti-
coats, hanging for sale in a profusion of pink and orange,
Prussian blue and peacock. The air was still heavy with the
scent of saffron and jasmine, myrtle and orange. Dark-eyed
maidens peered out of the folds of their *chadors*. Again, we felt
that Hafiz had been right!

It was in this idyllic setting that Tamerlane received bad news from home. One of his couriers, availing himself of the ever-efficient relay service of express horses, arrived from Samarkand to report that Tokhtamish, the Khan of the Golden Horde who had been driven from Tabrīz, had attacked Tamerlane's homelands of Mawarannhr from the north. Driven out of the Caucasus, Tokhtamish had executed an arc-shaped march eastwards through Russia along the north of the Caspian Sea and had now launched an attack directed against Bukhara and Samarkand itself. Tamerlane's own birthplace – the valley of the Qashka-Darya – had been penetrated by the Golden Horde. His eldest son, Omar-Shaykh, had only narrowly escaped capture in battle. The Jats had come, like pariahs, from further east to help Tokhtamish despoil central Asia. It was high time Tamerlane returned to look after his own.

The Qashqai on the move

The Gur Emir at Samarkand where Tamerlane is buried

Chapter 14

Migrating with the Qashqai

Tamerlane headed for home from Shīrāz. We were shortly to do the same. But we had one remaining ambition: to find and travel with the Qashqai on their migration. This nomadic tribe is reputed to have come to southern Persia only in the sixteenth century, and during Tamerlane's lifetime to have inhabited the region around Ardabīl (not far from Ahar from whence we had set out for the Qarabagh). Originally they claimed descent from the White Sheep Turkomen, that deceptively named tribe from eastern Turkey whose ferocious conduct in battle had achieved for them the distinction of being the only warriors to defeat Tamerlane. They seemed to us an integral part of his story, and the fact that they were still travelling – with their womenfolk, their tents, their horses and their flocks – much as Tamerlane had travelled, and in the same direction, made them a fitting objective for our final endeavours.

During our days in Shīrāz, we found the Qashqai much in evidence and not easily overlooked: the men in their strangely shaped felt hats, with ear-flaps sticking up like the wings on Mercury's helmet; the women in their brilliant multi-coloured and multi-layered dresses adorned with gold ornaments. Their

M

reddish skin and high cheekbones give the Qashqai the appearance of better-looking cousins of Red Indians.

From time to time in recent centuries the Qashqai have swept down from the hills to occupy the city and intimidate the citizens of Shīrāz; as recently as the 1950s, they staged a peaceful take-over at a moment of political crisis. Now they looked very much the country cousins in the metropolis, sitting in colourful but disorientated groups, or wandering perilously through the noisy, eager traffic.

It was the third week in May and we knew that the great annual migration, from the low-lying pastures south of Shīrāz to the summer hill grazing north-west of the city, must be nearly over. Those we saw in Shīrāz must have been left behind in one of the many encampments in the surrounding countryside. We thought it would be a relatively simple matter to find out the route of the main migration and hire a Land Rover to find them. We could not have been more mistaken.

Not since our frustrating day at Ahar had we encountered so much courteous obstruction. We talked to the Governor's office and to the administrators of tribal culture and education. We left not a waiting-room chair un-sat-upon, nor a glass of tea undrunk in any bureau in Shīrāz. We were offered visits to tribal school projects in or near the city; we were shown displays of tribal rugs; we were invited to lectures on tribal customs; we were even told we could go to Firūzābād, where the Qashqai had spent the winter and had been until recently. In fact, we were told everything we wanted except where to find them now. We were stifled with politeness and had the not unfamiliar sensation of swimming against a tide of cream.

Time and patience, those two universal panaceas of the East, brought their rewards. Eventually we met Rosie. Like Moghim on the bus to Alamut, or Eduardo at the hotel at Ahar, she was

clearly *dea ex machina*: the answer to a traveller's prayer. Rosie
was English – very English, in fact. Her husband worked in the
steaming heat of the Gulf at an installation which, as Rosie put
it, 'had no facilities – whatever that may mean – for European
wives'. So she was living in Shīrāz on her own during the week,
and teaching herself to weave carpets on a Qashqai loom. She
had visited the Qashqai several times, had been allowed to
photograph them and had worked out on a large-scale map the
routes which she reckoned they took on their migratory ride.
Best of all, she had a Land Rover.

Rosie immediately entered into the spirit of our quest. She
explained that the Qashqai liked to keep as far as possible from
the roads and from inhabited areas where they might be
accused of poaching grazing. As it was now the end of their
migration, they would have scattered into smaller groups. It
would not be easy to track them down: we could but try.

So we set out at first light one morning, taking with us all
our luggage, as much transportable food as we could buy
in the bazaar, Rosie's great dane and a few spare jerry cans of
petrol.

We took the road towards Ardekan and once we had put
some thirty miles between ourselves and Shīrāz, we started
looking in earnest. This involved leaving the Land Rover by
the road and scrambling to the crest of the nearest ridge to see
whether, in the valleys beyond, there were tell-tale plumes of
dust from moving camels, horses, mules and sheep. Again and
again we were disappointed. Sometimes our disappointment
was mitigated by seeing small clusters of black tents in the
distance. These – Rosie told us – were probably stay-behind
parties of Qashqai who had dropped out of the march either
because of lame animals, or because they had found a tempting
pasture where they wanted to linger for some days or weeks.

We could see through our binoculars that every tent seemed to have a dog: Rosie explained that these long-haired, woolly animals frequently acted both as guard dogs and as sheep-dogs, and that they had their ears cropped as young puppies in the belief that this would make them hear better.

After several hours of combing hillsides, we decided to take a rough track off to the west of our road and try to get into a different fold of country altogether. The Land Rover coped manfully. Eventually we saw an unusually large cluster of black tents beside one of the rare streams in this dusty, scrub-covered land. We headed straight for it.

The first thing that struck us as odd about this particular encampment was that the only animals were horses and the only humans were men – all wearing the distinctive Qashqai cap. The second curiosity was that all the men were of roughly the same age.

We stopped and, employing a few well-worn phrases, asked if they knew where the migrating Qashqai might be found. Were they still to the north-west of us? And had they any idea how far away? No answers were given. Instead, the men withdrew into the largest of the tents and a lively consultation ensued. Meanwhile, I recalled apprehensively Freya Stark's explanation that the laws of nomad hospitality 'are based on the axiom that a stranger is an enemy until he has entered the sanctuary of somebody's tent'. Would we be invited in?

To our utter surprise, the man who emerged now addressed us in English. Who were we? Where had we come from? Were we from the government or a television company? Apparently satisfied with our answers, he had a further rapid chatter with his companions. Then, to our great relief, he suggested we should join him under the shade of the black awning that was his tent. We sat down. He admired the great dane. A kettle appeared from the shadowy interior recesses of the tent. The ritual of hospitality had begun.

The explanations followed. This was not a Qashqai left-behind party; it was an advance party. They had ridden ahead of their fellow tribesmen to find a camping place, and at any moment they expected to be joined – not by the entire tribe (there are still about half a million Qashqai) but by a small horn of the general advance. If we wanted to see the Qashqai on the move, all we had to do was sit there and watch the skyline. In a state of happy anticipation, we unpacked our picnic and passed it round; the diffidence with which the Qashqai helped themselves contrasted strongly with the snatching of our First Muleteer in the Elburz.

We did not have long to wait. The Qashqai start their marches in the early morning and may cover anything between five and twenty-five miles in a day; but they prefer to find their camping places by midday if they can, and then spend the rest of the hot day in tending to the flocks, milking the ewes, making curds to be laid out and dried in the sun, and – if the time permits – assembling their looms and continuing work on their tribal rugs.

We saw the camels first. On the crest of a distant skyline we could discern black bundles and long poles: these were the tents hoisted high on the leading animals. One of the things the Qashqai have in common with Tamerlane's hordes is that they carry with them everyone and everything that belongs to them. As they got closer we could observe men on fine-looking horses, children on donkeys, packages on mules and – in addition to the tents – a bewildering variety of animate and inanimate objects on the camels. Many of these had brightly coloured rugs over them and, clipped into the folds of the rugs with long pins resembling knitting needles, were assorted objects secured one above another: a live chicken, a new-born lamb, a black iron cooking pot, a clutch of tent pegs, and – here and there – a well-wrapped-up Qashqai baby.

It is not infrequent for babies to be born on the migration, and while the immediate family may stay behind in their tent for a day or two, like the smattering of left-behind parties we had seen, they soon catch up the main body and the new-born babe becomes a cherished part of the tribal gear. 'Born in a tent – die in a battle' is an old Qashqai saying, and certainly from their earliest days Qashqai babies are expected to demonstrate hardy qualities. Until recently it was not uncommon, we had been told, to find weakling babies abandoned on the steps of mosques or hospitals in Shīrāz, having been left there by Qashqai mothers who doubted their infants' capacity to survive the rigours of the migration and the hard life of the tribe.

The cavalcade was getting closer to us. We could now discern the flocks of sheep bringing up the rear under the direction of fluffy dogs and barefoot children. Soon the leading camels were collapsing on their front knees and going through the curious contortions that constitute sitting down. This was a moment of intense activity, and the English-speaking member of the advance party suggested that we should stay in the tent and keep out of the way. He himself passed quickly on his horse among the heads of families, saying no more than a word here and there.

Like a well-disciplined army, the Qashqai pitched tent. Where a moment before there had been an open patch of hillside, suddenly there was a patchwork of black tents. But there was nothing military about the tents themselves; these were not bell-tents or bivouac tents, but awnings stretched at apparently haphazard angles attached to poles of unequal length. Outside the tents, the family's horses and camels were tethered or hobbled, while young lambs were unpinned from the camels' backs and either reunited with their mothers, or slipped inside the tents to join the children. We were later to learn that when the mares foal, it is usual for them, too, to be granted the privacy and protection of the family tent.

We had spent much of the past two months visiting the scenes of Tamerlane's exploits: castles and bridges, battlefields and conquered cities, mosques and grisly minarets. But never until now had I felt so close to the Tartar Horde as here, among their historical enemies, watching the process of nomadic life unfold.

It was time for introductions. Our English-speaking friend asked Rosie and Caroline to stay in the tent while he took me to meet the head of the principal family among this echelon of the tribe. We sat under the black goat-hair, cross-legged, sipping the ubiquitous glasses of tea. My host explained, through our new-found friend, that he was not the *Il Khan* – the head of the whole tribe. No longer did the Qashqai move as in former times, all in one body under the vigilant eye and firm command of their *Il Khan*. Now families moved in smaller groups and took their own decisions about their camping places and their pastures. They were discouraged from carrying firearms and no longer did they hunt as they did when he had been a young man. But – he added with a twinkle – they still had clear eyes and steady hands. (I was reminded of a remark made by a Qashqai to Marie-Thérèse Ullens de Schooten when she visited them twenty years ago: 'If I see, I kill . . . if I don't see, I don't shoot.') If we really wished to see something of his people, and of a part of Iran known to very few Iranians and fewer foreigners, and provided that we could ride, he had no objection to our travelling with his family for a few days.

I raced back with the good news of our invitation to Rosie

and Caroline. Alas, Rosie could not stay and had to go back to Shīrāz; her husband was returning from the Gulf. We wanted to accompany her all the way back to Shīrāz, but she was adamant that she only needed an escort as far as the road, being accustomed to much longer drives alone with her great dane. She had a remarkable send-off: fourteen Qashqai horsemen rode flanking her Land Rover, for all the world as if she had been in a state landau trundling down the Mall with its out-riders of Household Cavalry, till she reached the tarmac. We were sad to lose her.

Once again we were on our own in a strange land among strange people, too far from any habitation to walk there, even if we could have carried our luggage – which we couldn't. We were entirely dependent on the goodwill of our com-panions, and we felt in very good hands.

The Qashqai camp was a hive of activity. Young women, who had been spinning as they rode their donkeys, now set up more substantial looms at the entrance to their tents. Boys and dogs were rounding up recalcitrant animals. Small girls were collecting any scraps of brushwood or dry mule droppings with which they could make a fire. Old women were unrolling their renowned Shirazi rugs in the larger and more opulent tents, while others were unrolling brightly coloured *gelims* in the more humble tents.

When we returned from a wander around the camp, our English-speaking friend was waiting for us by a tent which had already been pitched for us. Our bags were laid out on a geo-metrically patterned rug, oddly reminiscent of Caucasian rugs until one remembered that the Qashqai were believed to have themselves lived for centuries on the fringe of the Caucasus. Kipi (for this was the nearest we could get to our friend's name) sat with us and told us simple stories of men and beasts.

His horse had a white blaze on its face, which meant that it was called a *Qashqa*; there had always been many such horses among the tribe which was why they were known as Qashqai (or Kashkai, or Gashgai or any of a myriad different transliterated spellings). His camel was known as 'the nose' because once it had led his family to a spring when they had lost their way on the migration and when all the flocks were thirsty. His brother was known as 'the unlucky one' because once his flock had been frightened by a wolf and had rushed into a ravine and killed themselves; but he was not unlucky any more because all his cousins had given him lambs and now his flock was almost as large as before. (We subsequently heard that this sort of voluntary rescue operation is a regular feature of life among the Qashqai, where individual misfortune is generally shared – so far as is possible – by the whole 'family'.)

Caroline started to prepare our evening meal from the provisions we had brought, but we could not persuade Kipi to stay and eat. He said he had to get back to his family tent. Instead, we were accompanied during our dinner by a circle of small Qashqai children who lay on their tummies watching us under the flap of the tent. We were reminded of our honeymoon in the Sahara, when we had found ourselves observed at night by a circle of Tuareg children's eyes staring out of the desert darkness under the brails of our bell-tent. In both cases, we probably presented a new phenomenon to our avid spectators.

The next few days' march was to be on a north-easterly bearing. By travelling with them we would be taking the line which Tamerlane himself had taken at the outset of his homeward march. For the first time on this journey, we were mounted on camels the following day. Around us were the pack camels with their black canvas loads. In front of us were the horsemen in their distinctive felt caps. Far out on our flanks were small parties of mules and riders looking like refugees flee-ing before some conquering force, which in a sense – since civilization and settlement were overtaking them – they were. Behind us were the donkeys with the old folk, and the flocks attended by the children and dogs. Some little groups were a mixture of all these elements. The Qashqai were on the move again.

When Tamerlane reached this point he had been campaign-ing for nearly three years. His memories must have been a strange compound of revelries and hardships, of glorious hunts and gory battles, of feats of courage and acts of treachery, of widespread destruction as a prelude to feverish construction in his native Samarkand on his return.

We had been travelling for only a few months, but already our memories, too, were a strangely woven fabric of contrasts. We thought of the uncertain footholds of the Rock of Alamut; the majestic dome of Soltānīyeh reaching up to an Islamic heaven; the cavernous markets of Tabrīz; the distant view of the plains of the Qarabagh stretching into the Caucasus; the black basalt walls of Diyarbakir; the blue waters of Lake Van below its mighty castle; the mountain fastnesses of Luristan; the brilliant mosaic tiles of Isfahan; the imperial columns of Darius's Persepolis; the orange groves of Shīrāz . . . all these and many more memories of an antique land. Always our eyes had been on the next horizon, the next dusty road, beyond which

> Gleams that untravell'd world, whose margin fades
> For ever and for ever when I move.
> How dull it is to pause, to make an end . . .

When unable to communicate with our guide over the Elburz mountains we had endlessly repeated the name of our destination to him: 'Shahsāvar, Shahsāvar!' we had intoned, as an incantation to keep him on the chosen path. Now I longed to go on as we were: riding into the sunrise, the noses of our camels pointing towards Samarkand. I longed to call across the sand to our guides:

> Lead on, oh captain of the caravan, lead on . . .
> We take the golden road to Samarkand.

This suspension of reality could not last. Soon we would have to say farewell to the Qashqai and fly home to our own country. But even before doing so, even before the day was out, our euphoric sense of well-being had turned to harsh anxiety and discomfort. By afternoon fatigue had replaced the zest of morning; the Qashqai had become spread out; Caroline and I had fallen behind and were separated from our guides and friends; my camel was lame.

In fact, I was lost in a strange land and nightfall was approaching. I was hungry and my provisions had fallen unobserved from my saddle somewhere behind me on the Persian plains. My throat was dry . . . my camel had just made a determined effort to bite off my left knee-cap . . . I had sand in my hair, my socks, my money-belt . . .

In my beginning is my ending. For us, the campaign was over.

Chapter 15

Epilogue: Samarkand and After

For Tamerlane this particular campaign was over too. But it was not the end of his career: far from it. He was to go home to defend, reorganize and beautify his capital of Samarkand, and then to undertake even more ambitious ventures in other directions.

As soon as Tamerlane had heard of the devastation which the Golden Horde were inflicting on his own homelands around the Oxus, he dispatched an advance column of his army to evict the invaders. Having settled the management of Shīrāz, he followed himself with the main body of his Tartar troops. As at Tabrīz and so often before, the mere rumour of his coming was enough to put his opponents into rapid retreat. Tokhtamish raised the siege of Bukhara and withdrew his forces northwards into the Kipchak steppes of Russia. Though Tamerlane was determined to pursue him and administer retribution, his first concern was to restore morale in Samarkand and along the banks of the Oxus.

He enquired into the circumstances in which his son had been defeated by the Golden Horde, and decided that the blame lay largely with an emir who had failed to show the expected degree of courage in the face of the enemy. This unhappy commander had his beard shaved off (a singular humiliation), had his cheeks coloured with rouge, was dressed as a woman and was made to run the gauntlet through the streets of Samarkand. The city of Urgench, close to Khiva, was razed to the ground and crops planted over the ground, to obliterate the memory of a community who had wavered in their loyalty.

There was worse in store for those who had abused Tamerlane's trust or been dilatory in his service while he had been away. A nobleman who had failed to return some of the horses sent to him for grazing was hanged; a wealthy merchant who tried to buy a reprieve for a corrupt administrator was hung by his feet; a butcher had his head cut off for overcharging the army for his meat; a mayor who had exploited the peasantry was executed. It was a curious inversion of European practice that in Samarkand the nobility were hanged and the plebeians decapitated: in no other way was Tamerlane a respecter of rank when it came to administering punishment. Clavijo, for instance, records that on different occasions a Tartar nobleman and his own dragoman were threatened – for comparatively minor offences – with having their noses drilled through.

But for those whose valour and devotion had not been impugned, there were celebrations and festivities on the return of the conqueror to Samarkand. We know much of the general appearance of the city and of the form the festivities took from the records of the two ambassadors who participated: apart from Clavijo, there was the energetic and observant Archbishop John of Soltānīyeh who returned to the court of Charles VI of France, bearing letters written in gold ink, after spending some time travelling with the Tartar court.

Largely as a result of the accumulation of spoils from foreign campaigns, Samarkand was already a splendid backcloth to such celebrations. Extensive areas of tented camps, gardens and the permanent pavilions of the wealthy merchants surrounded the walls and gates of the city. Through these last led the main highways from Persia, Afghanistan and the northern steppes, to converge at the centre of the town in an area of covered markets, mosques, caravanserais and palaces.

It was frequently in these private palaces that the most remarkable festivities took place, some of which were rendered exclusive to the more distinguished citizens by fairly drastic methods: lines of great wine jars marked off the feasting areas, and those rash enough to intrude beyond these lines without an invitation were shot down by mounted archers. The Tartar warriors and their ladies found nothing bizarre about continuing their revels with piles of wounded intruders around the periphery of the orgy.

And orgies they were. It was not unusual for the Tartar leaders' wives, including the Empress, to give dinners at which they methodically set about rendering their guests incapable through drink. Clavijo, who was both abstemious and censorious himself, noted this with amazement and dismay: he bad the greatest difficulty declining endless goblets of liquor, and recorded that when the Emperor handed anyone a goblet it had to be drained at a single draught. The self-discipline of the campaigning months was compensated for by the indulgence of the victory revels.

As with drink, so with food. Clavijo noted that the Tartars 'suffer cold and heat and hunger and thirst more patiently than any other nation in the whole world: when there is scarcity, sour milk tempered with boiling water suffices them ... but when food is abundant, they gorge on it gluttonously'. Indeed, Clavijo records elsewhere that a Tartar nobleman entertained him 'by roasting a horse whole with its head', to be followed by 'skins full of cream sweetened with sugar'.

The display of wealth in the pavilions and palaces of the great was calculated to dazzle. Not only did the great cathedral doors from Bursa – with their silver-gilt and blue enamel reliefs depicting scenes from the lives of St Peter and St Paul – adorn the entrance to the Empress's tent, but within was to be found such spectacular evidence of opulence as tent walls lined with ermine. There was a tree made of solid gold with fruit of balas-rubies, emeralds, sapphires, turquoise and pearls, and further adorned with gold and enamelled birds; the whole – we are told by Clavijo – was over the height of a man.

Indeed, the entire city of Samarkand was laid out to charm and impress the visitor. Clavijo remarked that it was a town set amid a forest: there were gardens and running water, fruit trees and cisterns, olive groves and aqueducts. But the charm was definitely secondary to the conscious effort to create the effect of an imperial capital: the encampments around were named after the great cities which Tamerlane had conquered or was to conquer – Soltānīyeh, Shīrāz, Damascus, Baghdad – as if to emphasize the subservience of these places to mighty Samarkand.

Tamerlane drove a great boulevard through the densely inhabited centre of the town, making a covered way with shops on either side. So impatient was he to see it completed, that he had the work carried out by shift-gangs working day and night. No truck was had with those who objected to the demolition of their homes, and no compensation paid to them, as Tamerlane claimed the whole ground space of Samarkand as his own private property. When supervising the construction of the congregational mosque, Tamerlane himself took up residence in the site, goading on the workmen from a perch on the scaffolding and tossing down scraps of meat to them as if he were feeding animals in a pit. His impatience to build and beautify his own capital was as overwhelming as his impatience to destroy the citadels of his foes.

It might have been thought that such rapid construction would as quickly decay. Indeed there were many who forecast that it would. Arabshah (the hostile biographer and captive of Tamerlane) reported that people feared to worship in the congregational mosque as stones fell from the roof so frequently; he considered the whole edifice damned because 'Timur built a mosque out of stolen plunder, like one who supports orphan children on the proceeds of harlotry'. But much of Tamerlane's Samarkand has, in fact, survived the ravages of time far better than might have been expected.

When I visited Samarkand from Moscow a few years ago, I was still able to see many of Tamerlane's feverish creations. The Bibi Khanum mosque, built between 1399 and 1401, did indeed crumble to a considerable degree during the hundred years following Tamerlane's death; but earthquakes contributed to this quite as much as any flaws in its construction. Even today the great duck-egg-blue dome, standing between shattered arches and minarets, evokes the glories of Timurid architecture.

But chief among the monuments of Samarkand today, and at any time of the past five centuries, is the tomb of Tamerlane himself – the Gur Emir. The interior is a splendour of gold, blue and white mosaic, under which the body of the emperor lies contained in a block of nephrite believed to be the largest in the world. This dark green, almost black, stone bears an inscription in Arabic to the effect that if the conqueror's mortal remains are disturbed, the whole world will tremble. It did not go unremarked that the week in which the Soviet archaeologist Gerasimov opened the tomb for the first time for five hundred years was also the week in which Hitler invaded Russia.

But to consider the disinterment – or even the death – of

Tamerlane is to jump ahead to the finale of a story which was far from its conclusion with the return to Samarkand after the three years' campaign of 1386–8. When he had set his own house in order, Tamerlane did not linger long before contemplating fresh conquests. Above all he was anxious for a reckoning with Tokhtamish and the Golden Horde. To this end, he pursued them across the Caucasian mountains to the banks of the River Terek, where the memorable night march and surprise attack which has already been recounted took place in 1395. After that encounter, Tamerlane pursued the remnant of the Horde along the banks of the Volga, the Don and the Dnepr – far into the heart of Russia. The Golden Horde never recovered.

In 1398, Tamerlane turned his attentions to India. Here the riches of the Hindu princes, coupled with the fact that they had – on occasion – sheltered his enemies, were sufficient reason for an invasion. Tamerlane crossed the Hindu Kush in deep snow, being lowered in a litter over the edges of precipices (from ledge to ledge in one case), and fought a number of engagements before arriving in front of the walls of Delhi. The battle that there ensued was preceded by the slaughter of some 50,000 captives (whom Tamerlane feared might cause trouble in his rear) and enlivened by the participation of 120 elephants on the Indian side. These redoubtable instruments of war – their flanks protected by heavy armour and their tusks fitted with poisoned scimitars – put fear into even the Tartar army. Tamerlane riposted by sending buffaloes and camels among the squadron of elephants, with lighted bundles of straw on their backs, which in turn put fear into the hearts of the elephants. One of Tamerlane's grandsons, a fifteen-year-old princeling, captured an elephant single-handed. The day was won by the Tartars, and the surviving elephants were made to kneel before their conqueror – who promptly dispatched them to Samarkand.

The city of Delhi surrendered, but – as at Isfahan – subsequent attacks by the citizens on Tartar soldiers set off a massacre of the inhabitants. More minarets of skulls were erected. In fact, the stench of bodies obliged Tamerlane to abandon the city and he set off for home by way of the foothills of Kashmir, frequently marching by moonlight or by torchlight and fighting as he went. Celebrations – in which the elephants participated – followed his return to Samarkand.

In 1400 – the year of the Dragon – it was the turn of the Sultan of the Ottoman Turks, Bayazid 'the Thunderbolt', who had struck asunder the united forces of Christendom at the battle of Nicopolis four years earlier, and who was now threatening Constantinople itself. Indeed, as Gibbon records, Bayazid boasted that he would not halt before Rome where 'he would feed his horse with a bushel of oats on the altar of St Peter's'. This was an opponent worthy of Tamerlane, particularly as Bayazid had already shown an inclination to threaten Tamerlane's conquests in Armenia and Eastern Anatolia, and to give succour to such old enemies of Tamerlane as the leader of the Black Sheep Turkomen. The first clash came at Sivas: Tamerlane undermined the walls and when negotiations for surrender ensued, he promised the defenders that he would not shed their blood. He did not – but he buried four thousand of them alive in pits specially dug for the purpose. It was a warning to Bayazid, and Tamerlane now allowed his attention to be deflected towards the Mamluk Sultans of Syria and Egypt.

Aleppo was the first of the Mamluk cities to fall. Tamerlane, using his captured elephants to good effect, overran the Syrian army and his supporters entered the city over a moat piled high with the bodies of fugitives. A contemporary Syrian account*

* By Ibn Taghri Birdi, whose father appears to have been present on the occasion.

describes the raping of the 'virgins and gentlewomen' of Aleppo
in disturbing detail. Tamerlane employed the captured Mamluk
princes on menial tasks, such as dragging provisions for the
army, thus no doubt inspiring Marlowe's concept of Tamerlane's chariot drawn by 'pampered jades of Asia'.

After Aleppo, the emirs of Tamerlane's army argued – not
for the first time – that their troops needed a rest. He scorned
the idea, and commanded an immediate advance on Homs,
Ba'albek and Damascus, doubtless urging his *tumans* on with
words akin to those put into his mouth by Marlowe on a different occasion about how to 'sustain the scorching heat' and make
'whole cities caper in the air'. The alarm at his advance was
extreme among the population of Damascus. An assassination
of Tamerlane was attempted but the assassins were detected,
with poisoned daggers in their boots, loitering around the
conqueror's tent. The daggers were tried out on their owners
and some of the would-be assassins returned to Damascus
minus their noses and ears. This incident, together with the
desertion of the Egyptian army sent to defend the city, decided
the governor of Damascus that surrender was imperative.
Tamerlane then 'misremembered' the amount of the ransom
the citizens had agreed to pay: no sooner had they gathered
up one sum than he insisted on a larger one until 'he had sold
Damascus to its people three times over'. Having thus sucked
all the wealth there was to be had from the citizenry, the town
was – on the slenderest of pretexts and despite all previous
assurances – given over to general pillage by the weary troops.
Ibn Taghri Birdi describes the sadistic behaviour of the Tartars
towards the population: 'they were bastinadoed, crushed in
presses, suspended head down . . .' Finally Damascus was set
on fire. Of all Tamerlane's enormities, his behaviour here was
probably the most grotesque. To the conqueror's question:

Behold my sword; what see you at its point?

well might Marlowe make the virgins of Damascus reply:

Nothing but fear and fatal steel, my lord.

Tamerlane had eliminated any threat from the Mamluks to the south-west of his empire: Syria was his, and the Sultan of Egypt quaked in Cairo. Pausing only to make a diversion to sack Baghdad, Tamerlane returned to his favourite winter quarters – the green pastures of the Qarabagh in the Caucasus – to rest his army and await reinforcements from Samarkand before his final trial of strength with Bayazid in Turkey. It was at this point in his career that the Christian kingdoms of western Europe first sent envoys to Tamerlane in the hope of enlisting him as an ally against their immediate enemy – Bayazid's Ottoman Turks; however, the Christians of Constantinople and further west, perhaps suspecting that Tamerlane would never prove to be a durable ally, neither sent to Trebizond the ships for which he asked, nor attempted to detain Bayazid's army at the gates of Christendom; they were glad enough of the temporary respite provided by Bayazid's requirement to protect his own rear.

Indeed, the two mighty Muslim captains now gathered all their hosts around them and advanced on each other. By cunning use of the greater mobility of his largely equestrian army, Tamerlane managed to arrive on the plains in front of Ankara with his army rested and refreshed; while Bayazid, whose largely infantry army had been chasing Tamerlane around the centre of Anatolia, arrived on the battlefield weary and to find the enemy occupying the better tactical position. Although one eyewitness★ calculated that the Tartar host numbered 1,400,000, more convincing estimates are that each army numbered some 200,000 warriors. A mighty battle ensued on the twenty-eighth of July 1402. Many of Bayazid's forces, disheartened by the poor pay in the Ottoman army and attracted by the celebrated generosity of the Tartar leader in the distribution of booty among his own troops, deserted to Tamerlane. However, the famous Turkish janizaries stood fast around their sultan and fought hard throughout the long day. At dusk, Bayazid decided on flight, but his horse was shot under him and he was brought a captive in chains before Tamerlane.

The chronicler Arabshah★★ describes how Tamerlane treated Bayazid with mock courtesy, inviting him to a banquet, dressing him in royal robes and having him served by beautiful veiled cup-bearers who, unveiled, proved to be his own wives and concubines. Bayazid not unnaturally attempted to escape, and thereafter was put in fetters at night and made to travel by day in a litter inside an iron grille – hence Marlowe's legend of his being caged like a wild animal.

With Bayazid's power broken, Tamerlane turned his wrath next on those Christian communities in Asia Minor which had helped some of the Turks escape to Europe, and which still held out against him. He captured Smyrna on the Aegean coast of Turkey, and it was then that he bombarded the fleet of the Knights Hospitallers using the heads of the slaughtered Christian knights as cannon balls. He declared his Turkish campaign a holy war on behalf of Islam and appeared to menace Constantinople as seriously as ever Bayazid had done. But already

★ Schiltberger, a Bavarian squire who was captured by Bayazid at Nicopolis and by Tamerlane at Ankara.
★★ See J. H. Sanders's translation of *Tamerlane* by Ahmad Ibn Arabshah (1388–1450), (London 1936).

his terrible gaze was turning eastwards again and Constantinople was to be spared for another fifty years.

For it was the Celestial Empire of China, under the sway of the Ming dynasty, which was to be the final objective of his last campaign. It was indeed almost all that remained to him of Asia to conquer; it was as if – in Marlowe's words – he had declared:

> Give me a map; then let me see how much
> Is left for me to conquer all the world.

The estimates of the size of the army which he led eastwards from Samarkand in the winter of 1404–5 range from 200,000 to 800,000; he was said to have taken provisions for seven years, and certainly he sent emirs ahead to supervise the planting of crops to feed his force on their way through. But it was not to be. The weather was bleak in Moghulistan that winter: the troops needed to drill four and five feet through the ice to reach the water of the rivers. The old emperor, in his felt-lined litter, suffered terribly from cold and imbibed spirits heavily to restore himself. His constitution, after years of campaigning and revelling, was not what it had been. On the plains of Otrar, north of Tashkent, on the eighteenth of February 1405 he realized that he could survive no longer. As so often, the last word – his last words – must be left to Marlowe:

> Farewell, my boys! My dearest friends, farewell!
> My body feels, my soul doth weep to see
> Your sweet desires deprived my company,
> For Tamburlaine, the scourge of God, must die.

Bibliography

ARABSHAH, AHMAD IBN (1388–1450): *Tamerlane*, translated by
   J. H. Sanders (London 1936)

BISHOP, MRS J. F.: *Journeys in Persia and Kurdistan*, 2 Vols.
   (London 1891)

BROWNE, E. G.: *A Year Amongst the Persians* (London 1893)

BURNABY, CAPTAIN FRED: *On Horseback through Asia Minor*,
   2 Vols. (London 1877)

BYRON, ROBERT: *Road to Oxiana* (London 1937)

CLAVIJO, RUY GONZALEZ: *Embassy to Tamerlane 1403–1406*,
   translated by Guy le Strange (London 1928)

EDMONDS, C. J.: 'The Travels of Arthur MacMurrough
   Kavanagh in Kurdistan and Luristan in 1850', *The Royal
   Central Asian Journal*, Vol. XXXVI (London 1949)

FORMENTON, FABIO: *Oriental Rugs and Carpets*, translated by
   Pauline L. Phillips (London 1972)

GIBBON, EDWARD: *The Decline and Fall of the Roman Empire*,
   Chapter LXV (London 1788)

HOOKHAM, HILDA: *Tamburlaine the Conqueror* (London 1962)

LAMB, HAROLD: *The Earth Shakers* (New York 1940)

LYNCH, H. F. B.: *Armenia – Travels and Studies: Vol. II, The
   Turkish Provinces* (London 1901)

MACAULAY, ROSE: *The Towers of Trebizond* (London 1956)

MACLEAN, SIR FITZROY: *Eastern Approaches* (London 1949), *A*

Person from England (London 1958), *To Caucasus* (London 1976)

MARLOWE, CHRISTOPHER: *Tamburlaine the Great* (London 1590)

MORANVILLE, H.: *Mémoire sur Tamerlan et Sa Cour par un Dominicain en 1403*, Bibl. de l'école de Chartres, Vol. 55 (Paris 1894)

PEREIRA, MICHAEL: *East of Trebizond* (London 1971)

PETITS DE LA CROIX: *Histoire de Tamerlan après le manuscrit Chereffedin Ali* (Paris 1722)

POLO, MARCO: *The Travels of Marco Polo*, translated by R. E. Latham (London 1958)

SCHILTBERGER, J.: *Travels and Bondage*, translated by J. B. Telfer (London 1879)

STARK, DAME FREYA: *The Valleys of the Assassins* (London 1934)

STEVENS, SIR ROGER: *Land of the Great Sophy* (London 1962)

ULLENS DE SCHOOTEN, MARIE-THÉRÈSE: *Lord of the Mountains* (London 1954)

WILLEY, PETER: *The Castles of the Assassins* (London 1963)

WILLIAMS, GWYN: *Eastern Turkey* (London 1972)

WRATISLAW, A. C.: *A Consul in the East* (Edinburgh 1924)

WRIGHT, SIR DENIS: *The English Amongst the Persians* (London 1977)

Index

Index

204